drawing for
fashion
designers

First Edition:

© March 2007 Parramón Ediciones, S.A.
Ronda Sant Pere, 5, 4ª planta 08010 Barcelona (Spain)

Company belonging to the Grupo Editorial Norma of Latin America

www.parramon.com

First printed in the United Kingdom in 2007 by

Batsford
10 Southcombe Street
London W14 0RA

An imprint of Anova Books Company Ltd

Pre-printing:
PACMER, S. A.
Printed in Spain

ISBN: 978 0 7134 9075 6

drawing for
fashion
designers

BATSFORD

4

Contents

Introduction

Fashion is the art of presenting an individual's personal appearance in public, and the cultivation of the image, though it also includes psychological and cultural influences, and even politics and philosophy. A carefully planned wardrobe makes it possible to attract attention to a particular individual, by enhancing our way of seeing that individual. The job of the fashion designer is to enlarge the scope of that wardrobe, diversifying, organizing, modulating and adding nuances to it.
The chief objective of fashion is to add impact to the presence of an individual, underlying the most attractive and striking aspects of their appearance.
It is not enough to create a design or pattern and simply repeat it time and again, but on the contrary it is necessary to constantly change and update styles in order to maintain an element of surprise.
   This constant renovation makes fashion into a kind of support for, or instrument of, personal expression, freedom and artistic creativity.

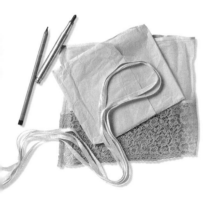

'Is fashion art? This question was first posed many years ago. But it does not concern fashion in itself. In fact, like the cinema, painting, music, literature, poetry, etc., fashion is an art when it is made by an artist …'

Pierre Bergé
Universo de la Moda
Ediciones Poligrafa

As in many artistic disciplines, fashion designers use drawing as an essential part of the creative process, as a preparatory piece of work that helps to clarify their first ideas and thoughts about form. Though many fashion designers work directly on the mannequin, it is hard to find anyone who completely does without drawing at the start, since the pencil strokes and areas of colour that flow across the page are the first allies of the imagination. Drawing, as an essential support for any artistic practice, is the only solid foundation on which the creative work of the fashion designer can be developed. The better the drawing, the greater will be the capacity of the fashion designer for communication and the better they will be able to visualize their own ideas.

A willingness to be open to the language of fashion drawing and familiarity with the artistic materials involved will help you to decide on the most appropriate way to express yourself for the project you have in mind.

Drawing is a useful means of inspiration for the fashion designer and as an expression of a characteristic style that can also be applicable to fashion books, magazines and advertising in general. As well as projecting the artist's creativity, drawing for fashion design should include some technical features that offer practical information and make the image the starting point for the industrial dressmaking process. Though creativity may be inherent in the artist, knowledge of the techniques of fashion drawing needs to be acquired through a guided process of apprenticeship.

This book is intended to bring the 'craft' of drawing to people aiming to break into the field, from fashion designers and illustrators to anyone who feels the attraction of the fascinating world of style. The reader will become familiar with the drawing processes and techniques used in the creative phase of fashion design: figure drawing, constructing the fashion figure, use of art materials, colouring, familiarity with and representation of fabrics. The book is set out in a similar way to the syllabuses that are followed in courses in fashion schools. The themes and practical exercises are always accompanied by sequenced illustrations, photographs and examples to help you overcome any difficulties a design might present.

Ángel Fernández

Graduated in Fashion Design from the Lanca School of Fashion Design in Bilbao in Spain. He studied drawing and painting at the Museo de Reproducciones Artisticas in Bilbao. He did postgraduate studies in Fashion Design Women's Wear at Central Saint Martin's College in London.
For more than 20 years he has combined professional fashion designing (for fashion houses such as Mid-e, Divinas Palabras and Manuel Albarán) with teaching experience in schools of fashion and illustration. Since 1998 he has been a professor at the Catalan Fashion Institute in Barcelona.

Gabriel Martín Roig

Degree in Fine Arts from the University of Barcelona, specializing in painting. Master's degree in museology and management of artistic, ethnological and cultural heritage from the department of History of Art, Social Anthropology and History of America and Africa of the School of Geography and History of the University of Barcelona. Postgraduate studies in coordination of contemporary art exhibitions with 'La Caixa' of Barcelona Foundation. His professional career has involved the publication of books on artistic techniques, the history of art and architectural heritage and teaching in art schools.

Selection and use of
materials

Pencils, paints

and papers

Familiarity with your drawing materials facilitates the interpretation of your design, improves your representation of character, your reproduction of the textures and the patterns of the clothing, and helps to give your illustration a sense of energy. All this allows your final design to be more easily understood, helping you to communicate better with your audience. In fashion drawing a wide variety of media can be used. In this chapter we are going to look at the media that are the most popular among professionals in the sector, studying them in all their various aspects and relating them directly to figure design. The greater your mastery of your materials, the better your drawing projects will be.

Graphite pencils

When you think of drawing the first medium that almost certainly comes to mind is the graphite pencil, with all its grades, from the hardest to the softest. Pencil is the best medium for drawing monochrome figures with linear strokes that emphasize the outline.

A CLEAN STROKE

A graphite pencil is the most immediate and accessible instrument to use for beginning to draw any model. It is a naturally occurring form of carbon of a leaden grey colour from which the 'lead' in pencils is made. It is a smooth material and is therefore easy to erase, allowing for a clean, precise line. The only maintenance required for a pencil is to sharpen it.

INTENSITY OF THE STROKE

The firmness and expressiveness of the pencil stroke depends on two factors: the pressure exerted on the paper while drawing and the degree of hardness of the pencil.

The letters inscribed on the side of pencils indicate the grade of hardness of each pencil. Pencils showing the letter H, ranging up to 9H, are the ones that make the faintest stroke. These are used for the first stages of sketching. Pencils graded from letter B to 6B are preferred by designers who can give a character to their drawing stroke, since controlling the pressure exerted on the paper they can achieve both soft lines and dark, intense strokes.

There are different grades of graphite pencils; those marked with the letter B provide a darker grey, while those marked with the letter H give softer tones.

Mechanical pencils provide a fine, precise line. They are highly suitable for sketching or marking details

Though not very often used in fashion design, graphite is also available in cylindrical, square or hexagonal sticks of varying thicknesses, which are very useful for doing quick shading.

DRAWING FIGURES WITH PENCIL

Pencil tends to be used in the first phases of a project in the blocking in and formal resolution of the figure. In general a drawing tends to be done almost exclusively with lines. To give better finish to the profile of the figure, the artist should continually modify the thickness of the lines in order to obtain variety and break with the uniformity of the line. Remember that the angle of the pencil is crucial for this purpose; the more tilted the pencil, the thicker the line.

WORKING WITH MECHANICAL PENCILS

Mechanical or automatic pencils have a button that enables you to push out the required amount of lead as it is used up. Its use can be quite varied in the different phases of design. A mechanical pencil with a lead of 0.5mm can be used to sketch or scribble ideas in a notebook, while others with leads from 0.3 to 0.9mm, in addition to dealing with the initial phases of the drawing, allow for greater quality and precision in the details. Mechanical pencils also have the advantage of not needing to be sharpened. Like conventional pencils, the leads present the same variety of degrees of hardness.

Graphite pencils are useful for doing linear work in which the outlines of the figure and the clothing take on a great importance.

Pastels and conté pencils

Pastels are made up of dry, ground-up pigment mixed with a binder to form a paste that, when hardened, forms crayons or sticks. Pastels are the closest you can get to pure colour, containing scarcely any elements apart from the pigment. A Conté pencil is made up of chalk bound with gum and oil that allows you to draw with a thick, intense line.

SOFT AND HARD PASTELS

Pastel sticks are either hard or soft, depending on the amount of binder employed. Soft pastels are very fragile cylindrical sticks that crumble easily during use, leaving intense spots of colour on the paper. The smooth density of soft pastels creates rich effects. Hard pastels come in thinner, square sticks. Their consistency is like that of chalk, but more compact since they have a greater amount of binder. They can be used in combination with soft pastels and Conté pencils. They draw cleanly on the paper, do not give off dust and are easier to draw with than soft pastels.

The stroke of the felt-tip pen marks out the profile of the figure while the pastels add a note of intense colour to the sketch.

Soft pastels are available in the form of very fragile cylindrical sticks. Hard pastels offer better consistency for drawing and are in the form of square sticks.

Pastels offer a vast selection of saturated, intense colours with tones very close to the pure pigment.

HOW TO APPLY PASTELS

With the pastel technique you can work with both strokes and dots, but the professional usually softens both to obtain surfaces of velvety colour. Often, the best way is to handle the colour with your fingers, shading and extending it over the paper with your hand or with a rag, building up the image by means of dots and touches of direct colour. Thus the different tonalities are mixed directly on the paper, creating shadings or gentle colour transitions. These softened or smoky tones can be combined with strokes or hatching of linear strokes of great intensity that will give your design a vigorous appearance.

CONTÉ OR CHALK PENCILS

Conté colours are used for rubbing and produce an effect similar to that of charcoal. Due to their hardness they are used both to draw fine lines and for filling in extensive tonal areas. They can be combined with pastel sticks. In this way large tonal areas can be rapidly covered by using the pastel stick flat on the paper and the Conté or chalk pencil to outline the figure or highlight it with expressive strokes.

These are the two basic ways of working with pastel: combining hatching of strokes of different colours or mixing the colour on the paper using *sfumato*.

Pastel colours are at their best when they are used on coloured paper. The contrast accentuates the outline of the figure and livens up the colours of the pastels.

Chalk or Conté pencils give a thick, intense stroke. Black is most frequently used for outlining and white for brightness or highlights.

Coloured pencils

Coloured pencils provide subtle lines or vivid strokes of colour. They are very clean and require hardly any maintenance, apart from sharpening them from time to time. They are not much different in use from the conventional pencil. All you need to remember is that the lines cannot be smudged and their creamy consistency means they cannot be completely erased.

ADDING DETAIL TO ILLUSTRATIONS

Coloured pencils occupy a position half-way between drawing and painting, allowing the artist to colour while drawing. This is ideal for giving a sense of volume to an illustration or bringing out the quality and colours of your designs. Coloured pencils allow you to add a great deal of detail to your illustrations.

IDEAL FOR SMALL FORMAT

Coloured pencils are not suitable for large formats and are used to their best advantage on work in small and medium-sized formats, since the small size of the pencil lead and the softness of the colours does not allow for easy coverage of large areas. Nonetheless, the precision of pencil strokes allows for a very meticulous finish to illustrations that require a realistic representation of fabrics with the accurate drawing of folds, shades and patterns.

Many designers prefer to have a wide range of different colours to hand in order to avoid having to mix shades on the paper.

Coloured pencils are a useful accessory for studying the design of patterns on the garments.

To obtain a watercolour effect from strokes made with water-soluble coloured pencils, all you need to do is touch the surface of the paper with a brush dipped in water.

Watercolour sticks are available from some manufacturers. These sticks are suitable for use on larger-sized illustrations. They create thick, intense strokes that are similar to those of creamy pastels.

Coloured pencils are used in a very similar way to conventional graphite pencils. The former, however, add a note of colour to the sketch.

TYPES OF COLOURED PENCILS

There are two types of coloured pencils: conventional and oil-based. Conventional pencils are harder and provide a fainter stroke; oil-based pencils have a larger proportion of pigment and their stroke is more intense, which makes it possible to work with deeper and more saturated colours. Their only disadvantage is that the points are more fragile and wear down more quickly.

WATERCOLOUR PENCILS

For the fashion designer, watercolour pencils are more practical than conventional coloured pencils. They have a similar composition but include a soluble binder that causes them to dissolve on contact with water. A hatching of strokes can be dissolved by passing a moist brush over the coloured area, making it possible to incorporate watercolour techniques into the drawing.

Coloured pencils are a very immediate medium, giving subtle and high-quality effects to your illustrations.

Felt-tip pens and marker pens

To work in fashion design you will need a complete range of colours and types of felt-tip pens.

Working with felt-tip pens is the most modern hand-drawing technique and is especially appropriate for illustration or advertising projects. The working process is similar to that used with coloured pencils, and excellent results can be obtained by combining felt-tips and coloured pencils.

THE PRINTED IMAGE
Before computers, felt-tip pens were the medium most often used by graphic artists and interior designers to obtain effects that looked as close as possible to the printed image. The finish offered by felt-tip pens is clean and precise, with clear outlines and a final quality that can easily be reproduced by photomechanical means. This is because felt-tip pens have a polyester tip with tiny holes that permit the flow of ink to the end of the tip in order to paint with saturated, uniform colours, without changes of tone.

VARIOUS POINTS
Felt-tip pen tips can be conical, cylindrical, flat or in the shape of a brush. Fine-point felt-tip pens are the most appropriate for drawing the outline of the figure, and filling in details and textured effects. The harder the point, the better defined the lines, though with use the point loses some of its hardness. Pens with a broad point, also called marker pens or markers, in addition to offering colouring with saturated, clean tones, also make it possible to cover an extensive surface with great speed. Brush-tipped felt-tip pens offer great flexibility, permitting different thicknesses of line to be drawn, depending on the angle at which they are held.

Alcohol-based markers allow for clean, uniform colouring without any appearance of hatching. They are particularly suitable for photomechanical reproduction.

Felt-tip pens can be mixed to form glazes, changing the underlying colour with superimposed layers of colour.

Some felt-tip pens have changeable tips, which can be replaced with new ones when they are worn out.

ALCOHOL-BASED FELT-TIP PENS

Alcohol-based felt-tip pens are preferred by the majority of illustrators because the ink evaporates and dries quickly. Colour mixtures are achieved by superimposing one colour over another. Once dry the colour is indelible and so other colours can be superimposed without causing the underlying colour to run. Colours are semi-transparent, which means that they allow the optical mixture of colours on the surface of the paper by means of a glaze effect. The paper should always be white when using felt-tip pens.

FELT-TIP PENS WITH WATER-BASED INK

With felt-tip pens using water-based ink, strokes take longer to dry, and sometimes underlying colours can be altered when one is superimposed on another. One way to extend the ink into other parts of the paper is by moistening the strokes with a damp brush. The method consists of drawing with the pen and then applying a wash to the drawing to produce tones or shading with the ink that is spread by the wash. Some manufacturers sell felt-tip pens with water-based ink containing a pigment similar to gouache. These colours are completely opaque and produce very good results in work that requires blocks of solid colour.

Felt-tip pens are very good for working on designs with patterns and bright colours.

Moistening the strokes made by a felt-tip pen with water-based ink using a wet brush can achieve effects similar to watercolours.

Inks and brushes

Ink is a liquid substance with an intense pigmenting capacity. It is capable of producing intense marks, precise when it is used thickly, and sinuous, transparent and delicate when its intensity is diluted with water.

INDIAN AND SEPIA INKS

Indian ink, always black in colour, is thick and opaque. It can be purchased in liquid form in glass bottles of different sizes or in the form of sticks. On drying Indian ink has a lacquered appearance and does not easily dissolve in water. Sepia ink, which is brown in colour, offers the same features as Indian ink, though once dry it can be dissolved again by simply touching it with a brush moistened with water.

THE IMPORTANCE OF PREPARATION

Illustrations in ink can be quickly executed but require thorough preparation, particularly if the work is to be done starting with spontaneous strokes, which are practically impossible to alter. So if you wish to do an accurate drawing with pen and ink it is very helpful to do a light sketch first. Then the definitive lines are drawn in ink over the pencilled outlines. When the ink has dried the pencil lines can be erased.

When drawing with ink and a brush it is important to carefully control the pressure applied in order to vary the thickness of the line.

Indian ink in stick form requires more preparation than liquid inks but the results are of better quality.

Indian inks provide an intense, black stroke that gives a great graphic quality to your designs.

WORKING WITH THE BRUSH

If the ink is applied to the paper with a brush, working with the tip and using hardly any pressure at all, firm, sharp lines appear of variable thicknesses and a strong graphic quality. A sable brush with a good tip projects, in a single brushstroke, the rhythm and play of light of a subject. With a movement of the wrists and forearm you can easily change direction with the brush, turning and rounding corners where a pen or pencil would fail. It is important to control the pressure used with the brush to obtain different nuances and thicknesses of line. The ink reacts differently depending on the moisture and texture of the surface and the amount of water mixed with the ink. The more water the mixture contains the lighter will be the colour of the ink, and it will spread in a different way depending on the paper that is to be drawn on.

WORKING WITH TONES

Besides purely linear designs, sketches of a model can be made up of marks using different mixtures of water. If this is the effect you want, it is best to work with medium or thick brushes. Creating different tones of grey with ink is as easy as dissolving the ink in a little water or applying a wet brush to a mark, extending it until the tone gets lighter. In fashion design, drawings are seldom completely tonal. They tend to be combined with some strokes (done with a felt-tip pen or pencil or with a finer brush) that prevent the figure being excessively undefined.

Linear work done carefully with the tip of the brush is usually combined with light washes of a faint grey that give a sensation of shadow and volume on a dress.

Coloured inks and watercolours

The watercolour technique is based on effects of transparency created by pigment diluted in water when it is applied to the white surface of the paper. This same principle governs work with coloured inks, also known among designers as anilines or liquid watercolours.

COLOURED INKS

Coloured inks are available in a wide range of colours. Most of these inks are based on colouring agents made from aniline dyes, which produce a strong colour tint. The colours are very bright and saturated, so it is necessary to dilute them with water before colouring a figure. It is advisable to use distilled water for dilution since it improves the fluidity and quality of the illustration.

THE SOFTNESS OF WATERCOLOURS

Watercolours are chiefly composed of gum arabic, glycerine and colour pigments and, unlike inks, provide a range of very soft colours. The richness of tones does not just depend on mixtures of different colours but also on the amount of water used. Transparent watercolours can be made opaque or semi-opaque when mixed with Chinese white. Chinese white is a mixture of a zinc oxide pigment and gum arabic. It is a deep white that mixes to produce colours of a pastel tone due to its high degree of opacity.

There are many selections of coloured inks and anilines available. The fashion designer needs a good selection that includes a sample of each colour. Variations can be obtained later by using mixtures.

Inks for fountain pens and anilines produce interesting effects when mixed with a little bleach. The same results cannot be obtained with watercolours or other inks that do not contain aniline dyes.

The most attractive aspect of colouring with watercolours is the variety of the washes they offer, which result in fascinating textures in clothing.

COLOURING TECHNIQUE

In fashion illustration, watercolours and coloured inks tend to be used to colour and fill in shapes that have previously been drawn with pencil, Indian ink or indelible felt-tip pen (watercolours are seldom used in the construction of the drawing). When the first washes have been used to colour in the design, secondary colours can be added to highlight certain details. This is accomplished by intensifying the tones with a glaze effect, superimposing new washes over others that have dried. The most suitable brushes for working with inks or watercolours are those with a rounded tip, since they make it possible to cover an area quickly and at the same time to make very fine, highly detailed strokes.

Watercolours allow you to dilute colours to different degrees, which leads to subtle and harmonious effects.

Gouache and acrylics

Gouache and acrylics share many characteristics though their make-up is quite different. Both are water-soluble paints, although acrylic, once dry, is permanent and has a satiny sheen. Gouache, on the other hand, is much more opaque and once dry is matt and can be dissolved again by passing a moist brush over it. Gouache and acrylic should never be mixed together in the same work.

THE VERSATILITY OF ACRYLICS

This is the most modern painting medium and the most versatile, offering a choice ranging from opaque colours through to transparent glazes with a subtle finish. Acrylic paint is quick-drying, so one brushstroke can be applied on top of another without the colours mixing, allowing for very sharp superimpositions. Patches of thick, dry acrylic colour result in a satiny surface that looks like plastic, so it is not advisable to do impasto work that is too thick. If you are going to work with transparent glazes, it is better to mix some acrylic medium with the paint instead of a lot of water. This will prevent the colour losing strength and adherence.

Acrylic paint is a colouring medium that is very suitable for patterned garments with prints. Its quick-drying properties allow the designer to produce areas of colour with clear, sharp outlines.

If you paint with acrylics or gouache it is useful to have a selection of a few basic colours. The definitive tone of the colour is determined by mixing shades on a palette.

QUICK DRYING

Because of the quick-drying properties of acrylics it is possible to cover painted areas with new, opaque tones, and to correct and touch up the colouring as you work. This means that if you want to mix colours or gradations directly on the paper, you need to work with great speed so that the paints do not dry before you have finished. This is aggravated if the paper you use is thick and porous, rapidly absorbing the water the paint contains. Working with this medium it is possible to obtain effects ranging from the strictest realism to expressionistic and imaginative designs.

OPAQUE AND SOLID COLOURS

Gouache is an opaque paint so in theory it is possible to use light colours over dark ones. The superimposition of one colour over another can be complete and perfectly solid without leaving a trace of the underlying colour visible. However, in practice, it is better to stick to the method of dark colours over light colours since gouache is not as opaque as oils or acrylics. Given that the colours of gouache contain little binder they are still soluble when dry, so that an application of a colour will take on something of the colour of the layer underneath. To lessen the chance of this happening let one layer dry completely before applying the second one.

A MEDIUM FOR RETOUCHING

Gouache, like watercolour, is a water-based paint, though it is rougher, more forceful and less subtle and atmospheric. It should be applied like a cream; it is not a medium that is very appropriate for working with transparencies, so it is not advisable to add too much water to the paint. In spite of these drawbacks it represents an advantage for the fashion illustrator, as it permits all sorts of repeated modifications until the treatment, colour or texture suitable for each garment is obtained.

As a medium for retouching, gouache is almost indispensable, particularly for illustrations requiring a high level of finish and precise detail. Retouching of gouache is very easy to do and is scarcely visible in the finished work.

Since it is denser and more solid than watercolour, gouache allows for a treatment of colour that is more homogeneous and is thus appropriate for colouring in designs of prints with flat colours.

Gouache allows for a uniform treatment of colour in which scarcely a trace of the brushstroke is perceived, along with very vivid, slightly whitened colours.

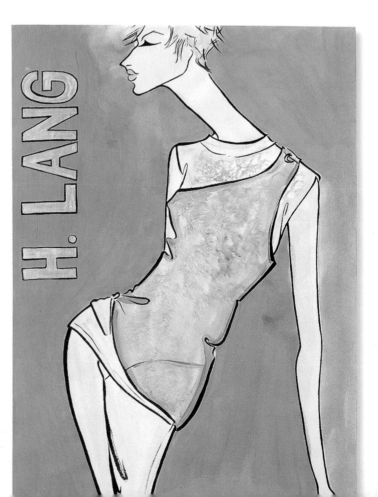

Surfaces for drawing: paper and sketchbooks

Paper is the most usual material for drawing among fashion designers, though for the presentation of a project it can be accompanied by samples of fabric and textures to complement the design. There is a great variety of different types of paper available, and the choice depends on the medium that is going to be used in the drawing.

FINE-GRAINED PAPER

It is possible to make clear strokes and lines on fine-grained and smooth papers, to develop a wide range of greys with graphite pencils and provide good results when working with both graphite and coloured pencils. Gloss paper is not suitable for coloured pencils, which do not adhere so well to the surface. Smooth papers without any texture are best for drawing with felt-tip pens. The felt tip should slide easily over the paper. The most suitable paper for drawing with felt-tip pens is layout paper, since it prevents the ink soaking into it and is 'bleed-proof'.

COARSE AND MEDIUM-GRAINED PAPER

Very coarse papers are not very suitable for fashion drawing since the pencil or brush stroke cannot penetrate the paper's grain and white spots can appear on the coloured areas, reducing precision and detail. Medium-grained papers are more frequently used. Canson paper is a highly recommended example of a medium-grained paper as it is moderately coarse and is available in a wide range of different colours.

Watercolour paint and pencils require special paper. The most suitable kinds of paper are those with a medium grain that are highly absorbent (made of cellulose, flax or cotton fibre). The most commonly used paper for watercolour painting has a weight of 250 g/m².

Papers most frequently used by the fashion designer: fine and medium-grained papers, tracing paper and different kinds of coloured papers (of medium and dark tones).

PAPERS WITH UNUSUAL FORMATS OR TEXTURES

If you are capable of creating fashion collections and styles, you can also apply your creative spirit to selecting an interesting format for drawing. Why not experiment with unusual formats, types or textures of papers? Working in this way could stimulate your creative processes and give your designs an original touch.

SKETCH PADS

Sketch pads are available in a wide variety of formats and qualities. The size of the page and the ease with which they can be carried and used are good reasons for choosing them. Sketch pads tend not to be used for projects, but they are very useful as a proving ground: for making travel notes, sketching initial ideas, pasting in photos of designs or pieces of material that you come across and especially like.

TRACING PAPER

This is used for copying. When doing a technical drawing it is common to draw only half the garment, and, if it is symmetrical, the other half is copied. Tracing paper is used to transfer a sketch to a final work and also to superimpose two drawings that contain different levels of information on the garment.

The selection of original types of papers on which to do your drawing can be a novel complement to your creations.

Stylizing the
human
figure

'MANY PEOPLE FEEL INTIMIDATED WHEN THEY WORK FOR THE FIRST TIME WITH A
MODEL, KNOWING THAT THE COMPLEXITY OF THE BODY, WITH ALL ITS LIFE AND
FLEXIBILITY, REQUIRES YEARS OF STUDY TO LEARN TO DRAW IT WELL. THE EVIDENT
DIFFICULTIES SHOULD NOT BE DISCOURAGING. JUST AS IN OTHER PROBLEMS IN
DRAWING, ONE CAN LEARN TO SIMPLIFY WHAT IS SEEN TO OBTAIN RESULTS THAT ARE
COMPREHENSIBLE.'
Rainer Wick. *Pedagogia de la Bauhaus*. Hatje Cantz, Germany, 2001

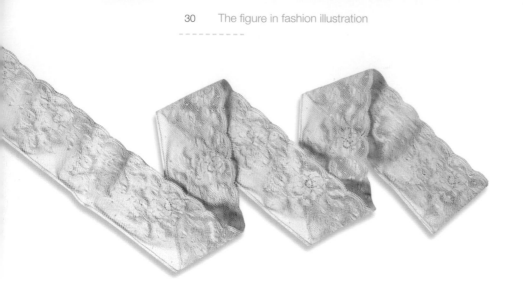

The figure in

fashion illustration

Familiarity with the proportions of the human body is an essential area of study for students of fashion. It symbolizes the search for and establishment of certain laws of beauty expressed by means of archetypes. The study of the canon (guiding rules) is vital for correctly drawing the figure and cannot be ignored no matter how much imagination and fantasy there may be in the design, since the garment must in the end be fitted to the human body. After analysing and understanding the harmonious representation of the human figure from an academic point of view, it is then necessary to learn how to stylize it. This means modifying some proportions of the body to adapt them to the language of fashion, while at the same time respecting the relationships between the different parts of the body.

The nude figure

How we look to others is the result of the anatomical structure of the body and all its expressive forms. Taking into account that as a fashion designer you must adapt the clothing you make to a figure, it is important to have a good understanding of the nude: the structure and proportions of the human body. Many people feel intimidated the first time they work with a model, knowing that the complexity of the body, with all its life and flexibility, requires years of study if one is to draw it well.

THE IMPORTANCE OF THE NUDE FIGURE

Drawing a nude figure represents more of a challenge than any other subject because the proportions, the coordination of the different elements and correctness of the pose reveal a reality that is very close to every person, so a mistake that in another subject might pass unnoticed will be obvious in this case. In spite of the highly stylized character of many fashion projects, designers today, however radically anti-academic they might claim to be, cannot totally do without using the nude human body for their representations, their stylistic reflections and artistic practice.

THE BODY AS THE FRAMEWORK FOR YOUR CREATIONS

Learning to draw the nude human body may appear to have little to do with designing creative fashion collections, but it will help you to get to know the possibilities and restrictions of the framework within which your creations have to be developed. Without some basic understanding of anatomy it is impossible to do a good illustration or clothing design, however innovative and stylized it might attempt to be. Any student of fashion should start out by learning to draw the nude figure. It cannot be stressed too highly that if you design clothes, whatever your sources of inspiration, you must always remember that you are designing for the human body. So practising drawing the human figure will always be an extremely valuable exercise.

LIFE DRAWING

The best way to tackle the nude is by life drawing. All art colleges offer students the opportunity to draw the nude figure from life. Signing up for some of these classes will always complement a fashion designer's training. Drawing the human figure from life provides constant training and endless possibilities for improvement for the artist. Life-drawing sketches are quick notations done in a few minutes. Through this exercise the hand acquires confidence at the same time as discovering different ways to portray any sort of posture or anatomical feature. Do not be discouraged by the apparent difficulties presented by life drawing. Just as in any other problem in drawing, you can learn to organize and simplify what you see to obtain excellent results.

There are many books available that are devoted solely to drawing of the human figure and to anatomy that help us to better understand the structure of the body.

Proportions of the body

The 'canon' of the proportions of the human figure is a code of guidelines using mathematical formulae to establish the ideal proportions of the human body, dividing it into sections called modules, which position the parts of the body and calculate their proportions.

THE CLASSICAL CANON

The proportions of the academic figure derive from the classical Greco-Roman canon. This is a highly standardized view of the body, which does not correspond to any particular individual but exemplifies the general ideal of the man, the woman or the child. The main use of a classical canon is to be found in the modules (eight for the height and two for the width in adults) that make it possible to compare the relationship between the different parts of the body. This system of modules also makes it possible to refer to other significant points that are helpful in understanding anatomy and facilitating the representation of the figure, as well as locating references to width in order to check on the most important elements of the outline.

THE HEAD AS MEASUREMENT

The size of the head plays a key role in the construction of the human figure in terms of proportion, since it serves as the basic module for measurement, namely the total height of an adult figure is eight times its size.

To draw a correctly proportioned figure the height of the head is measured. A straight, vertical line is drawn and this measurement is marked on the line eight times. From this vertical line straight horizontal rules are projected that permit the figure to be constructed. Once the drawing is finished the marks and measurements are removed with an eraser.

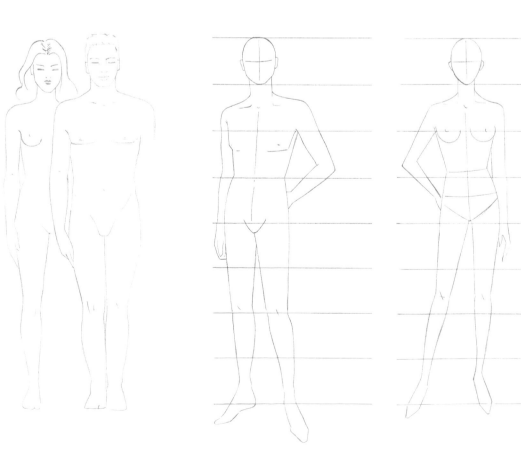

Male and female figures seen in front view, drawn using the module system, with a height of eight heads.

A 'SLIMMER' CANON

The canon of eight times the human head is valid for the study of drawing in general, but it is not the most suitable for representing the figure in fashion. In fashion design schools the canon for the height of the human body is eight and a half heads (for women) and nine heads (for men). This is for two reasons. The first is to make the body appear slimmer (though in the next section we will analyse how this reaches its ultimate expression in the stylization of the figure); and the second is the exceptional, above average height of most professional models. In addition, the female model is almost always presented wearing high-heeled shoes. In other words, the prototypical body of the fashion drawing is taller than in the classical, Greco-Roman canon.

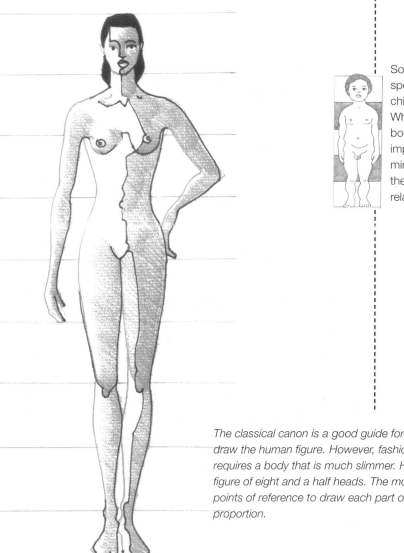

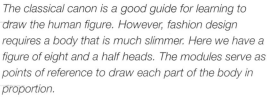

The classical canon is a good guide for learning to draw the human figure. However, fashion design requires a body that is much slimmer. Here we have a figure of eight and a half heads. The modules serve as points of reference to draw each part of the body in proportion.

Some designers specialize in drawing children's fashion. When drawing the body of a child it is important to keep in mind the larger size of the child's head in relation to the body.

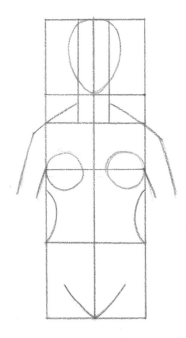

THE MODULES SUGGEST THE MEASUREMENTS OF THE BODY

When constructing a female figure of eight and a half heads using the system of modules, some anatomical points of reference can be observed that can be useful for drawing. The first module corresponds to the size of the head; the second indicates the level of the armpits and the top of the breasts; the third coincides with the elbows and the navel; the fourth marks the level of the pubis; the fifth the maximum length of the arm; the sixth the level of the knees; and the eighth the position of the ankles. It is important to remember this system if you want to draw a well-proportioned human figure.

The first four modules of the construction of the figure correspond to the head and torso. The lower extremities can measure between four and five modules.

Schematic lines and simplification of the figure

Schematization consists of simplifying the structure of the body by reducing it to a few essential strokes. This simplified way of working makes the figures easier to draw while still seeming correct, and it can be done without experience of drawing a figure from life.

An important aspect of becoming a fashion designer is knowing how to fill a page with figures drawn with broad, rapid and simplified brushstrokes or lines.

FROM THE GENERAL TO THE SPECIFIC

The secret of synthesis or simplification is to avoid anatomical details and focus your attention on the general form of the whole. In other words, you need to learn to work from the more general rather than the specific. The aim is to see the human figure as an articulated whole, focusing on the basic shapes of the torso, the head and the limbs and on the proportional relations that are established between them.

THE FRAME OF THE BODY

To construct a figure begin by projecting the internal skeleton in a very simple way. Reduce the body to a visual armature (as a sculptor would) made up of very simple curved lines (as if they were wires). They should give visual form to the principal structures such as the line of the shoulders and hips and the segments that indicate the position and length of the extremities, marking the joints with small circles. You end up with a geometrical figure that looks like a robot and that shows the essential structure of the body.

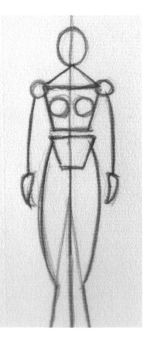

The head is an oval, the neck a triangle, the torso and hips are simply represented with two inverted trapezoids, the shoulders and breasts are circles and the extremities are curved lines.

GEOMETRY OF THE HUMAN BODY

Another way to deal with the complexity of the representation of the human figure is to use simple geometric forms that are moulded to the structure of the body, working with them until a convincing, recognizable structure is obtained. The human body represented by volume is composed of spheres, cylinders, trapezoids, ovals and triangles. These forms contain the essence of the shape. It is a matter of combining and articulating these shapes to build up the form of a body in proportion.

WHERE TO START FROM

The first problem that any beginner faces on drawing the human figure is: where to start? The answer is to start by drawing the head, then the neck and then, working downward, draw the shoulders and the torso, which should form a gentle trapezoid. The breasts start below the armpits. Another trapezoid constructs the hips. Finally add in the lower and upper extremities (in that order).

The figure can be constructed as if it were made of wire. The torso and the extremities appear defined with curved lines that shift as the posture of the body changes.

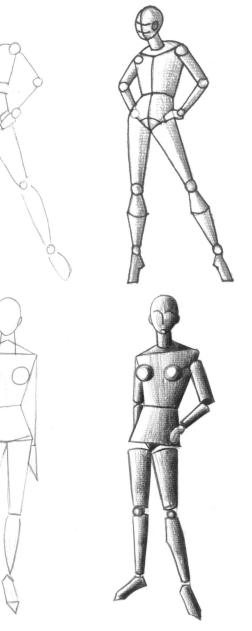

The process of construction of a visual armature for the human figure by using lines should be the first step towards transforming the body into a solid representation.

The human figure can be broken down into simple geometric shapes that establish the pose and the proportions of the parts of the figure. After that light shading is all that is required to give them volume.

The fashion figure

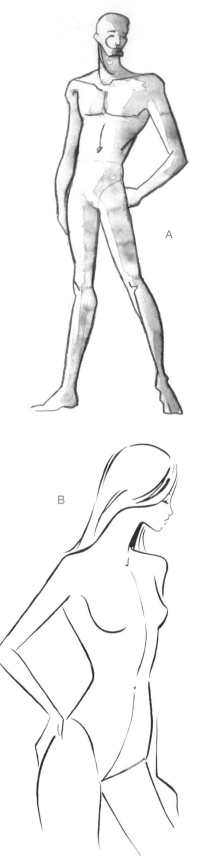

The previous chapter was concerned with the study of the internal structure of the body; this one will look at the exterior outline, which defines the anatomy: the shape of the 'fashion figure', the name given to the schematic representation of the body in fashion drawing.

THE OUTLINE OF THE FIGURE

Drawing the outline of a figure is an extremely interesting exercise, requiring attention to be centred on the boundaries of the shape, paying no attention to any detail or shading effect. A good way to start is by drawing the outline of the body from the top down. Begin with the neck and then draw the gentle slope of the shoulders. From there, go down the body to trace the curving shapes of the muscles. Draw a geometric, jutting line if the model is male and a lighter, sinuous line when drawing a female body.

RELIEF IN THE OUTLINE OF THE BODY

The outline of the body is determined by its underlying muscle formation. Going down from the neck, this can be represented with a curve that points towards the inside of the body, while at the shoulders it points outwards. The same outward curve occurs at the elbow. The arm and forearm show curves that turn inwards. The hip forms a generous curve swelling outwards that ends at the knee, where the line makes a slight inwards curve. The calves curve sharply outwards. At the ankle the line marks a more pronounced curve, first inward and then outward.

The form and directions of the curves of the outlines of the body should be studied carefully in order to correctly construct the fashion figure.

The profile of the male fashion figure is characterized by a pronounced musculature and straight, emphatic lines (A). The female figure has a sinuous line, delicate details and a silhouette in which the curves are predominant (B).

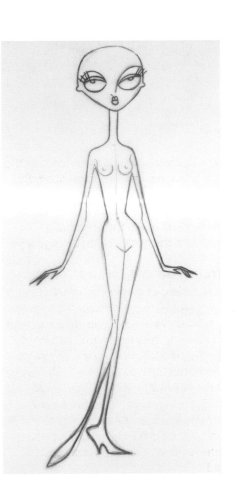

In the teaching of drawing it is always recommended, in order to avoid difficulties in representing the outline of figures, to draw in the empty spaces – in other words, the background that surrounds the figures.

Once you have designed a fashion figure whose silhouette and pose you like, you can trace it onto tracing paper and use it several times, dressing it in different clothes, as if it were a doll.

THE FASHION FIGURE

The fashion figure is the graphic representation of the model. It is built up around a line drawing that emphasizes the pose and the most striking curves of the outline of the figure. If you do not have much experience in drawing, remember to use a faint stroke, since the drawing will always involve some corrections or superimposed lines. Once the form is finalized, mark the lines that are essential in order to see the contours, but do not erase the rest because they also constitute an integral part of the study. When the figure has been completed, a sheet of tracing paper can be used to trace the simple outlines of the figure, then this template can be used again and again.

CONTROL OF THE STROKE

The fashion figure should have a lively expression and the line should be clear enough to give all the information necessary to understand the pose and the anatomy of the model. To make the line interesting the designer needs to combine different thicknesses of stroke. To do this you can vary the angle of the pencil to modulate the line or alternate the pressure and angle of the brush. A good exercise to help you to learn to modulate the line is to try to do a figure with a single continuous line, without lifting the point of the pencil from the paper.

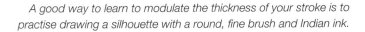

A good way to learn to modulate the thickness of your stroke is to practise drawing a silhouette with a round, fine brush and Indian ink.

Stylizing the figure

In fashion design a realistic presentation of the figure is often dismissed in favour of a more stylized and idealized vision of the model.

Formal exaggeration is common among fashion designers and illustrators, and to achieve it, some liberties need to be taken with the proportions of the body.

A DRAWING WITH STYLE

A design should have an impact on the client, not just because of its originality but also thanks to a stylized illustration. For this reason every professional should have a characteristic drawing style that is unique to him or her and, in addition to creating style and immediate impact, should be capable of linking in with the general style of a fashion collection in a clear and effective manner.

This means getting away from the discipline of academic drawing, without forgetting the basic ideas of the structure of the human body that have been previously examined in this book. Keeping these basic ideas in mind, you will find it easier to stylize your drawing.

ELONGATING THE FIGURE

To make your figure more stylized, all you need to do is to elongate some parts of the body. The first step is to make the head slightly smaller, and the neck thinner and longer, while the proportions of the torso are scarcely altered and the legs seem longer. If the intention is to increase the height of the model while maintaining a correct proportional relationship between the different parts of the body, you need to increase the height of the body from one to two modules (figures of nine or ten heads).

If you follow this format, the anatomical relationships are the same though the lengths of the extremities and of the principal body masses have been modified.

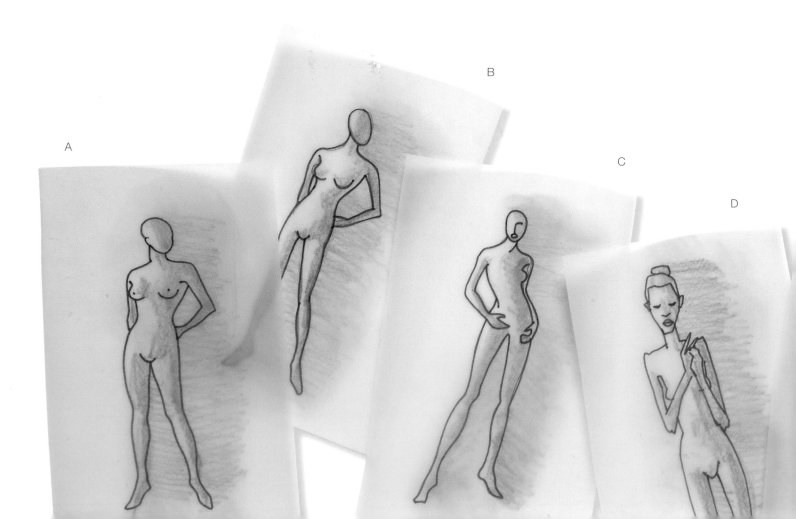

A

B

C

D

SLIMMING THE FIGURE

Another option for accentuating the stylization of the figure is to reduce the muscle mass. This method attempts to make the figure look slimmer without making it taller, leaving the basic proportions unaltered. The waist and hips are narrowed, the pubis seems a bit higher than its usual position, the legs and arms are of the same length but are thinner, the neck is more slender, and the head and feet keep their initial volume, so they are perceived to be larger in relation to the proportions of the rest of the body.

TAKING LIBERTIES WITH PARTS OF THE BODY

When the basic structure of the figure is correctly proportioned, the designer can take some liberties, such as altering the proportions of certain parts of the body in order to personalize the figure or impose a drawing style that is more in keeping with the design of the clothing. Current trends include exaggerating the size of the head (like a doll), enlarging the size of the eyes (as in *manga* animation) or giving the anatomy a tremendous flexibility (as if it were a rubber figurine).

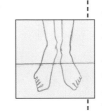

Half a module can be added to the legs, at the base of the feet. This increases the slimness and elegance of the leg and makes it possible to view the design and the form of the shoes more clearly.

Stylized models have a powerful presence. The body is elongated to highlight the garment and leave more space for the creation. The styling of the figure should be in relation to the garment being shown.

To stylize the body, enlarge it to a size of nine or ten heads. The neck seems longer, the shoulders are slightly wider in comparison to the pelvis, the torso is shortened and the legs are stretched out. The length of the feet is kept in proportion with the height of the body.

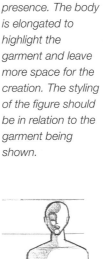

E

F

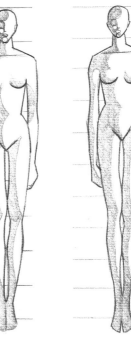

Different examples of stylization of the figure (from left to right): a figure of eight heads, Greco-Roman canon (A), the same figure made thinner (B), figure of ten heads (C), figure of nine heads made thinner (D), exceptionally stylized figure with distorted proportions (E), stylized figure with big head (F).

Studying the

pose

Designs for garments would look predictable, static and lifeless if no attention was paid to the posture or pose of the figure. The energy and dynamism inherent in the figure is captured and revealed in the posture of the body. To make it come to life it is not enough just to understand anatomy; you also need to give the figure rhythm, vivacity and 'spark'. In the field of fashion design it is vital to pay close attention to the habitual movements of fashion models, who should act in harmony with the style of clothing that they are wearing. Presenting an outfit or creation correctly depends to a great extent on the appropriate choice of a pose for the figure.

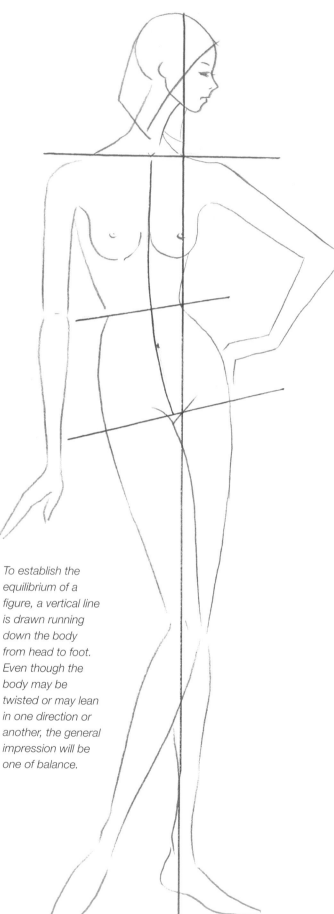

To establish the equilibrium of a figure, a vertical line is drawn running down the body from head to foot. Even though the body may be twisted or may lean in one direction or another, the general impression will be one of balance.

Balance and rhythm

A convincing balance and use of the rhythmic potential (the dynamic tensions within the figure) are fundamental to the stability and credibility of the pose. Maintaining the balance at the same time as highlighting the rhythmic lines of the figure makes for a sense of restrained movement and adds a greater emphasis and dramatic quality to the pose.

TENSIONS CREATE BALANCE

The balance of the figure is the most important factor to consider when drawing an upright posture. The image should be quite erect; if not it can give the impression that the body is about to fall over. The best way to test the balance of a figure is to imagine a vertical line running along the central axis of the drawing, from the head to the floor. Any inclination of the shoulders is counterposed by another in the pelvis and legs in the opposite direction. In this way the figures appear portrayed in a strange equilibrium that is dominated by action, in a constant, interrelated movement.

A good way to learn to capture the rhythm of a figure is to make very quick sketches that hardly give you time to think. The results will be much better if your model is in motion.

Once the curves that define the rhythm of each pose have been located it is a good idea to exaggerate them for greater emphasis. The figure, though slightly disproportionate, will gain tension.

DETERMINING INTERNAL RHYTHM

For a figure to achieve an impression of balance and rhythm an internal line should be imagined that marks the direction of the pose, an imaginary line that runs along the figure to affirm its rhythmic effect. You can attempt to discover this rhythmic line (also known as a 'power line') by superimposing directional curves on drawings or photographs of the model. These structural lines should become a point of reference for any designer; they are a basic linear scheme from which any pose can be constructed in a convincing way.

EXAGGERATING THE CURVES OF THE BODY

Mastering this line is very important because, apart from defining the specific outlines of the volumes of the figure, it establishes a sense of direction or vital impetus and creates tensions and reactions, and special rhythmic cadences in the figure. To construct a pose in a dynamic way you need both to exaggerate the curvature or inclination of the rhythmic lines and to accentuate the curves that shape the outline of the body. This allows you to give more of a sense of energy to an apparently rigid and conventional pose.

QUICK POSES

A good way to practise with rhythm is to try drawing poses in just a few seconds. By using a minimum amount of time to complete each pose you will end up with images that capture the essence and the overall gesture of the body, in fluid drawings, full of life and spontaneity. Do not be afraid to make mistakes.

When drawing fast, some of your sketches will inevitably not come out well, but others, in contrast, will have a freshness that can be lost when an idea is worked on too much.

To begin with it is necessary to individualize the key line – the curve that describes the rhythmic structure of each model. This line can take a number of different directions, since each posture has its own basic rhythm.

The importance of the torso

The basic structure of the torso can be represented as a trapezoid and the hips present a trapezoidal or triangular form. These are the basic geometric forms to use when drawing the body.

Proportionally, the torso occupies two and a half modules in the canon of the female figure. This part of the body has a great importance in helping to give purpose to the model's pose, so this chapter will study it in detail.

STRUCTURE OF THE TORSO

The basic form of the trunk is composed of two mobile structures: the thorax (between neck and abdomen) and the pelvic region. Both areas are represented with a trapezoid shape, one for the torso (inverted) and one for the pelvis (slightly flattened). In profile it can be seen that the thorax tends to lean forwards and the pelvic region backwards. The shape of the breasts of the model can be similar to an inverted wineglass and the dimensions vary depending on the model's physique, while the abdomen describes a curve that ends at the base of the pubis. To reproduce the masses and movements of the body accurately, you need to understand this structure in terms of two articulated parts.

SHOULDERS AND PELVIS: OPPOSING TENSIONS

The pelvis is connected to the shoulders by means of the spinal cord, forming the axis of the body. Thus it is logical to suppose that any inclination of the shoulders will affect the position of the hips. Each bend to the side at the hips will be accompanied by a move in the opposite direction by the shoulders, while each movement of the shoulders is followed by a shift of the pelvis. In other words, if the shoulders lean to the right the natural reaction is for the hips to lean to the left; so the body is always in balance. This pose is known as *contraposto*.

This is another way of structuring the torso. It can be helpful to draw the torso and the hips as two forms that are articulated independently.

The line of the shoulders and the line of the hips always lean in opposite directions. It is important to be aware of this effect to correctly represent different postures.

THE SPINAL COLUMN IS THE AXIS OF THE BODY

When analysing the torso from the back you can see that the spinal column is the axis of the body, since it constitutes a line of symmetry from which fundamental measurements are established. On drawing it you can take as a point of reference the different parts of the body, being aware that the correspondences and the measurements of the organs that you draw on both sides of this line should be the same. This knowledge is useful for learning how to draw the torso. Nonetheless, in fashion design the pose taken from the back, particularly a rear view, is a not a subject that is often used.

CARRYING THINGS IN THE HANDS

Fashion figures are often shown accessorizing the garment they are wearing with items that modify the attitude and posture of the torso. This is the case with bags or hats that are held in the hand. Though the object in question weighs very little, styling calls for the accessory to pull the body downwards in order to draw the viewer's attention to it. Thus the shoulders lean to one side and the arm is extended to hold the object in the hand, and the body corrects this weight by leaning to one side. The marked inclination of the hips acts as a counterweight to the slope of the shoulders.

The way professional models walk fascinates and enthralls with its seductiveness and elegance. This is represented by exaggerating the inclination of the lines of the shoulders and hips, always in opposite directions.

When the torso is represented from behind the curve of the spine appears as a vertebral axis.

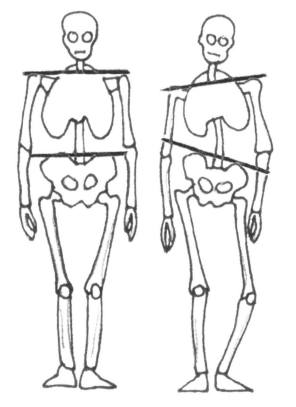

The skeleton confirms how the inclination of the hips brings about an inclination of the shoulders in the opposite direction.

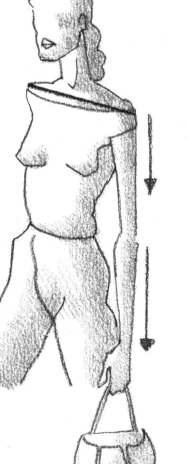

When the model carries a handbag or other accessory, even though it does not represent a significant weight, the body is slightly inclined to emphasize its presence.

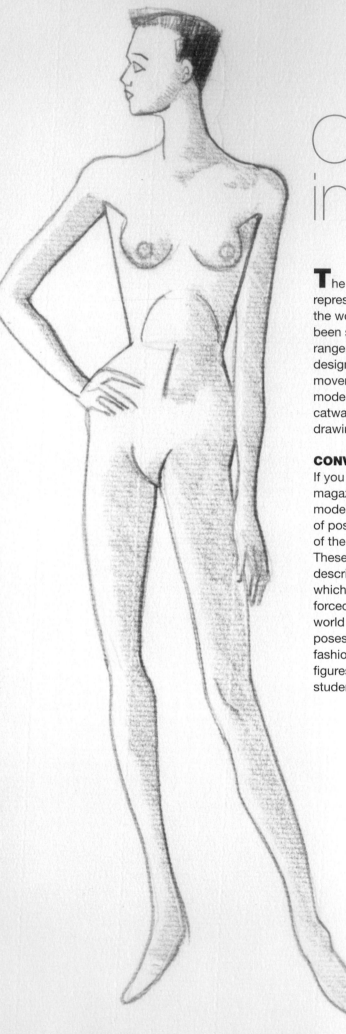

Common poses in fashion design

The drawings on the following pages represent the most common poses in the world of fashion. These poses have been selected from among a wide range of different positions, and are designed to give a summary of the movements most often used by models when they parade down the catwalk and by designers when drawing figures.

CONVENTIONAL POSES

If you flick through any fashion magazine you will notice that the models photographed repeat a number of postures, which have become part of the universal language of fashion. These postures and gestures can be described as conventional poses, which some may suggest as being forced, unnatural and exclusive to the world of fashion. These conventional poses are also very commonly used by fashion designers when drawing figures, so it is a good idea for the student of fashion to get to know and use them too, adapting them to his or her own style, since in the field of design they have a generally accepted, universal meaning assigned to them.

FITTING THE POSE TO THE STYLE

A person's posture is a product of their cultural and professional background, age, sex, state of health, level of tiredness, etc. It is a good idea to take into account the psychology and status of the client for whom the garment is intended before deciding on the posture your model is to adopt. If your dress is an haute couture garment, the pose will be sophisticated and elegant. If you are designing fashion for young people, the model should be shown as dynamic, using more informal and even provocative poses.

This posture, in which all the weight of the body is put on one leg and with hand on hip, is probably one of the most recurrent poses in fashion design.

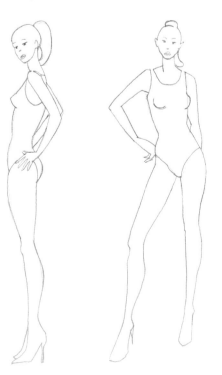

Here is a selection of some of the most common poses used in drawing fashion figures. Often photographic models are a good point of reference for drawing the figure.

THE KEY IS IN RELAXATION

In selecting postures for your fashion figures you should avoid full-frontal poses and too much rigidity and symmetry. You will know when you have selected the right pose for your figure when you feel that it is harmonious and graceful, and it appears to be a relaxed representation. Relaxation appears in the asymmetrical position of arms and legs, in an inclination to one side, in the correct inclination of the line of the shoulders and hips, in the relation of hand and arm, and in the balance of the body when the subject leans forward or backward. Unnatural postures and jerky-looking movements should be avoided.

STUDYING POSES IN THE WORLD AROUND US

The best way of finding suitable postures for your projects is by trying to sketch figures of personalities who appear in magazines or by drawing people you see in the street (a man leaning against a lamppost, a group of young people sitting down, a girl waiting…). You can learn how to indicate with a few strokes a graceful movement, a confident attitude, a charming gesture or an agile movement. Fill your sketchbooks with different poses. Later you will be able to use them for illustrations for catalogues or magazines. You will be surprised how quickly you can sketch the pose of a figure once you have acquired enough experience.

Here is a selection of conventional postures in the field of fashion that every designer should have in their pictorial repertoire.

Arms and hands

The arm is the upper extremity of the body and is made up of four moving parts: shoulder, arm, forearm and hand. Though the arms and hands have an assigned proportion in the canon in relation to the rest of the body, the stylizing tendency of fashion design can alter their dimensions as long as they harmonize and fit in with the whole.

A SIMPLE SCHEME

To represent the arms, start with a simple diagram that shows their correct articulation. The best way to draw an arm is to construct it using superimposed circular shapes or cylinders if you wish to bring out its volumetric form. Then, on drawing the outline, pay attention to the prominent muscles, the greater volume of the shoulder, the biceps and the forearm (particularly when dealing with a male arm).

The female arm is very different from that of the male and should be drawn more delicately. It is characterized by the absence of prominent muscles, the regularity of the proportions and the delicacy of the outline. In female arms the areas of the joints at the elbow and wrists are narrower than the joints in the male arm.

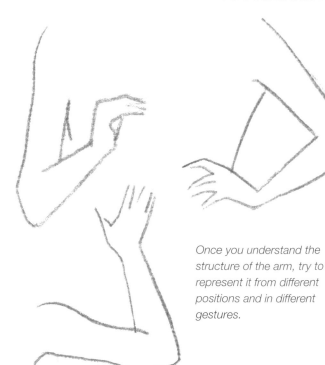

To draw the arm, start with a straight line that acts as an axis or juxtapose different circular shapes to suggest the arm with its articulations.

Once you understand the structure of the arm, try to represent it from different positions and in different gestures.

The arms cannot be understood in isolation. The best way to represent them is interacting with the body. They emphasize its posture and contribute rhythm and asymmetry to the figure.

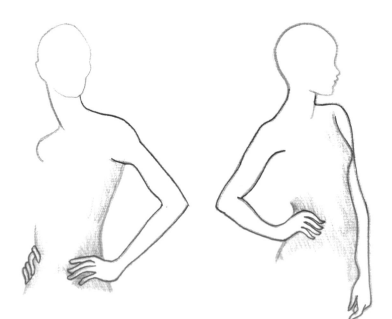
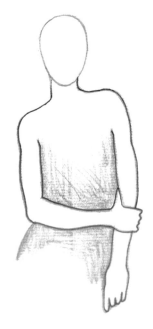

DRAWING THE HAND

The hand is the part of the body that can take on the greatest number of different positions, so it represents a certain amount of difficulty for the inexperienced draftsperson. A well-drawn hand gives the figure a graceful finishing touch, while a hand that is badly drawn can damage good work. Two aspects need to be considered: the back of the hand, where the tendons end and knuckles start; and the palm of the hand with its more rounded shapes, since here the more fleshy muscles are to be found.

STARTING FROM A STRUCTURE

To better understand the dimensions of the hand, start with a geometric scheme of the outline and then continue with a representation of the fingers using lines or ovals.
The length of each finger is different. The different points of articulation and movement are indicated with a slight curve of the line defining the fingers. This is because their position corresponds to a scheme composed of concentric arches.

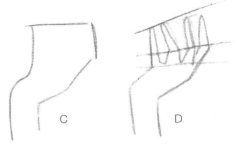

The structure of the hand is simple: it is divided into two halves, one corresponding to the palm and the other to the fingers (A). The positioning of the fingers is drawn with various curved lines that coincide with the points where the knuckles flex (B). Though the structure of the hand is simple, drawing

it becomes complicated when the fingers open and grasp. In such cases it is inadvisable to portray them using a geometric form (C). Lines are drawn over the geometric form to show the extension of the knuckles and with them the shape of the fingers is concluded (D).

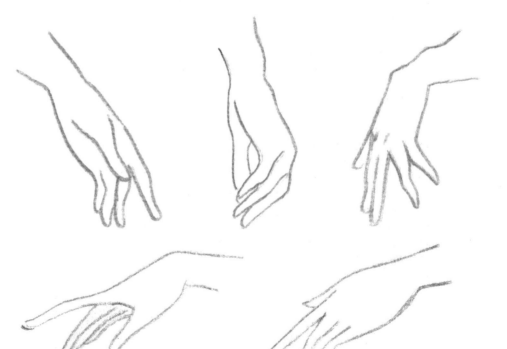

After studying the structure of the hands it is a good idea to draw them in different positions. Use models from magazines or books or do drawings from life.

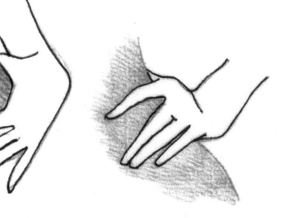

There are two positions of the hand that call for special attention: when it is partially introduced into the pocket, looking for a support, or when it is resting on the hip.

Legs and feet

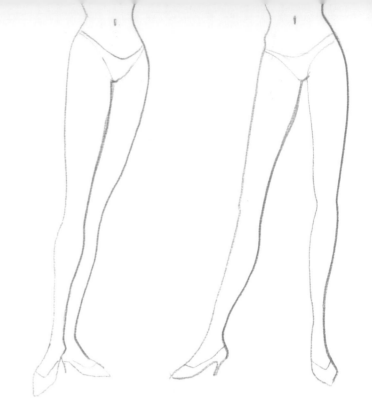

Though they have the same number of joints as the arms, legs and feet offer fewer possibilities in terms of variety of movements. This is because the joints of the hips and ankles only permit flexing and extension (and not lateral movement) and the knee does not permit movements equal to those of the arms. As a result, legs are easier to draw than arms.

Female legs present a sinuous outline, with gentle curves that should be drawn without hesitation, using a single continuous stroke.

LENGTH AND JOINTS OF THE LEG

Proportionately speaking, the leg, along with the foot, occupies four modules of the total canon of the figure. It is made up of three moving parts: the thigh, the lower leg and the foot, joined by the joints of the hip, the knee and the ankle. The length of the thigh and the lower leg is the same.

As with the arms, the structure of the leg can be represented by superimposing circular and elliptical shapes. With female legs the shape of the muscles is not very marked, and their outline is sinuous, the muscle delicately narrowing as it approaches the knee. The lines are gentle and not pronounced, so that the circle formed by the knee should scarcely protrude. In the lower part of the leg the calves taper down to the heel. They become more rounded and gain in volume when the model wears high heels.

To draw legs correctly it is essential to bring out the curve of the muscles and the narrowness of the knee and ankle.

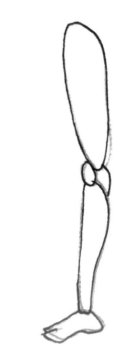

The leg can be simplified to two elongated shapes with rounded outlines that join at the knee. The foot has a triangular shape.

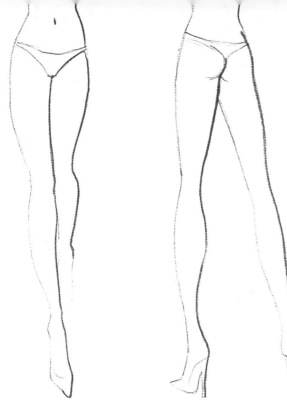

High-heeled shoes bring out the volume of the calves and create a curve that is greater than usual.

The divergent position, which is quite common for representing figures in fashion, is the representation of the legs when they are pointed in different directions. For example, one foot is shown in profile and the other in front of it in three-quarters position. This means that one leg is drawn from a side view and the other frontally.

LEGS WITH HIGH HEELS AND LEGS CROSSED

Models' feet are often dressed in high-heeled shoes. They give the instep a highly pronounced curve. This kind of footwear gives the leg elegance. The rise of the heel with respect to the toes contracts the calves, which show a more pronounced curve from the ankle to the back of the knee. When drawing a seated figure, the length of the legs, particularly if they are crossed, should be depicted as longer than usual. Otherwise they may seem too short.

THE FOOT, CLOSED AND COMPACT

According to the canon, the length of the foot is equivalent to an eighth of the height of the body and thus equivalent to the height of the head. In contrast with the hand, the foot presents a volume that is more closed and compact. The scheme of the drawing is similar to that for the hand. In other words, you start with a circle or oval that corresponds to the heel, another, more elongated oval for the metatarsus and various lines or small cylinders to represent the toes. If the foot is represented in profile a triangular shape is enough to show its basic structure.

Once the structure of the foot is understood, the next step consists of drawing it in different positions. In the front view the toes become simple circular forms.

Very often fashion figures wear high heels. However, some designers prefer to depict models with flatter shoes.

The position the foot takes with high-heeled shoes tenses the toes, which curve to form an important point of support.

Drawing the

head

For a student starting out in fashion design, the head is usually one of the more complicated artistic subjects. This is the part of the body that has the most variety in terms of form, volume, proportions and expression. For this reason the head deserves individual analytical study. In this chapter the basic aspects of the study of the head are reviewed: knowledge of its structure, the proportions between the dimensions of the different parts and key suggestions on how to work up your design from an original sketch. Then the different parts that make up the head are analysed, along with the possibilities for stylization and the degrees of distortion that fashion design permits.

Proportions of the head: front view and profile

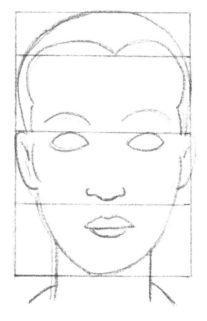

In the classical canon the human head is three and a half times the length of the forehead. The sections correspond to the hairline, the level of the eyes, the base of the nose and the chin.

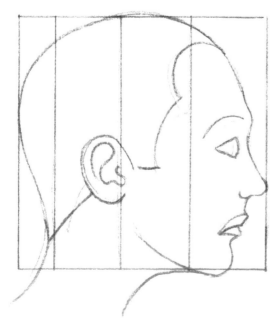

The head in profile can also be divided into three and a half parts, corresponding to the back of the neck, the location of the ears, the point where the neck begins and the tip of the nose. The horizontal lines are the same as those for the front view.

One of the most important sections in any study of the human head in figure drawing is the one that deals with the problem of proportions. To draw the head correctly it is essential first to understand its structure and academic proportions. From there on, each designer can use this knowledge to stylize the drawing and achieve his or her own style.

THE SIZE OF THE HEAD

According to the classical canon the human head is three and a half times the length of the forehead, so the height of the head is divided into three and a half units. However, in fashion drawing there is another, more stylized set of proportions, which divides the height of the face into four equal parts. The first corresponds to the hairline, the second to the level of the eyes, the third to the base of the nose and the last to the chin.

THE FACE FROM THE FRONT

The shape of the head is like an egg, with the upper part made up of the cranial cavity and the lower part consisting of the mouth and jaws. The head, seen from the front, is symmetrical, and that line of symmetry is a first point of reference for the artist. If you draw in this vertical line that divides the face in two you can establish an axis of symmetry to enable you to position the features in proportion.

THE HEAD IN PROFILE

In this position the head presents a more rounded shape than from the front view. In the classical canon it is divided into three and a half parts, but for fashion drawing it is acceptable to draw a vertical axis that divides the head into two equal parts and will serve as a point of reference on which to situate the ears. The canon established for the head seen from the front also serves for the profile. The same horizontal divisions that are applied to the head as seen from the front coincide in the profile with each of the different parts of the face. The eye in profile is drawn as a triangle. The triangle is also the most suitable geometric form for the basic shape of the lips.

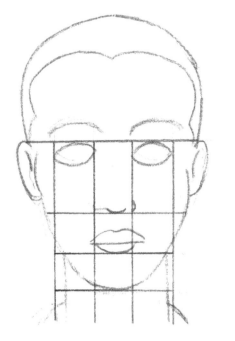

If horizontal and vertical straight lines are projected on the face as viewed from the front you will find a number of correspondences and measurements that can serve as points of reference for drawing.

The human face is a complex subject. To draw it well requires plenty of practice. Why not carry a small sketch pad to practise on whenever you have some free time?

MEASUREMENTS OF THE FACE, FRONT VIEW

In the face there is a relationship of sizes and measurements between the different features that must be taken into account. The face can be divided vertically into three segments that are equal to the width of the eyes. Between both eyes there should be enough space to draw a hypothetical third eye. That same space determines the width of the nose. The eyes should be at the same level as the ears. Horizontally, the face is divided into three sections. The section on top is twice as wide as the lower sections because it is determined by the length of the nose. The two lower sections show the position of the mouth and of the chin. Add the arch drawn by the eyebrows to the elements described above and you have a scheme of a drawing that is suitable for representing the head and its features.

THE SCHEME OF THE HEAD

Once you have understood the academic canon of the human head, it is time to put into practice what you have learned. It is possible to simplify the form of the head using an oval. On it a vertical symmetry axis is drawn. On this vertical straight line the facial features are indicated with four lines that correspond to the hairline and the levels of the eyes, nose and mouth. The level of the eyes should be at the centre of the head. On these lines you can draw in the different parts of the face schematically.

Another system of measurement suggests that the head should be divided into eight modules, two for width and four for height. The vertical axis helps construct the head in a symmetrical fashion. Here, this method is applied to three different poses of the head.

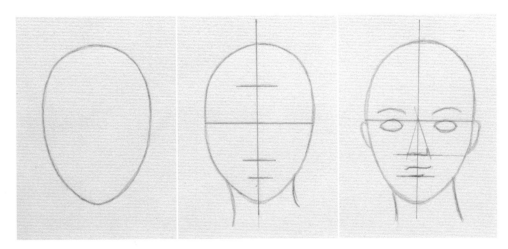

Once you have understood the academic proportions of the human head you can learn to synthesize what you have learned with a few basic measurements and the use of simple geometric shapes. The drawings here show the process of synthesized construction.

Stylization of the head

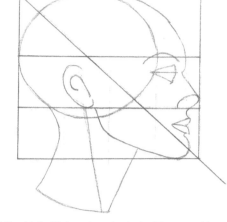

To construct the Nefertiti-type head, start with an oval head framed by a square that is divided into three parts indicating the levels of the eyebrows, the nose and the chin.

The stylization of the head is a controlled distortion, the partial disproportion of some of its elements in order to bring out a style or feature you want to emphasize. To familiarize yourself with this process, some of the more usual options for stylizing the head are shown here.

THE NEFERTITI TYPE

This is so called because it recalls the features seen in the portrait busts of the Ancient Egyptian Queen Nefertiti in the realist style that was popular in the reign of her husband Akhenaton. The Nefertiti type is characterized by an elongated, egg-shaped head, a prominent chin, fleshy lips and a long, thin neck. This Egyptian ideal of beauty has endured to modern times among fashion designers. Its structure is based on three rectangular modules that indicate the levels of the eyebrows, the nose and the chin. Inside this box a circle is drawn that outlines the cranial vault, with a head that is slightly elongated in the direction marked by the diagonal line. The drawing is completed on the basis of this structure, with a long, slim neck.

THE TWIST OF THE NECK

In fashion drawings a twisting or elongation of the neck is quite common. The musculature and mobility of the spinal column gives it great flexibility. Thus the neck complements the expressive quality of the torso, breaking the symmetry established by the spine with an inclination that is opposed to that marked by the elevation of the shoulders (if the shoulders lean to the left, the head leans to the left, and vice versa). This gives more grace to the figure and accentuates the rhythms of the body.

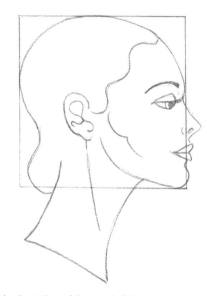

The diagonal orientation of the oval of the head makes the chin more prominent, which, in turn, contributes to stylize and lengthen the drawing of the neck.

Sketchbook with different examples of stylized heads of the Nefertiti type. The style is characterized by the twist of the neck, its length and thinness.

TYPOLOGICAL SCHEMES

The different shapes of the head can be grouped into basic typological schemes that the process of stylization will accentuate by means of progressive distortion. It is possible to transform the basic shape of the head (an oval) and distort it so that it takes on a circular, rhomboid, square, triangular, rectangular or almond shape. You can experiment by first drawing your chosen geometric shape and then attempt to draw the head inside it, as if it were a box, adapting the curved outline to the rigid shape that encloses it.

STYLIZING THE FACIAL FEATURES

Once the stylized shape of the head has been drawn, the features can be added. Search for elegance and distinction in the position of the head, grace in the movement of the neck, character and purpose in the expressive force of the glance, etc. Any of these features can transform the appearance of the head with a longer neck, fleshier lips or bigger eyes. So the parts of the face (nose, eyes, ears, mouth, chin, lashes, eyebrows …) can be modified individually, thus helping to personalize the stylized drawing.

After deciding on the degree of distortion and the shape of the head, the features (eyes, nose and mouth) should also be stylized and adapted to the style chosen.

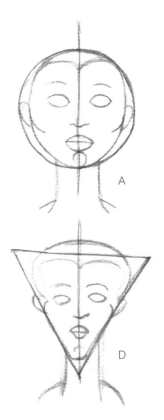

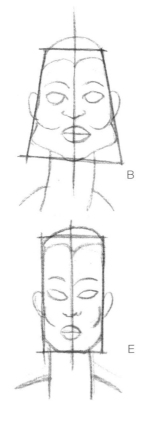

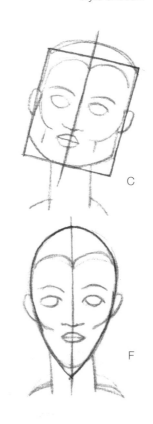

The typological scheme determines the degree of distortion and the shape that you wish to give the stylizing of the head. Here are different typological examples of heads: round (A), trapezoidal (B), square (C), triangular (D), rectangular (E) and almond-shaped (F).

The eyes and nose

Different types of eyes can be developed by modifying the shape, the length of the eyebrows or the size of the pupils.

The parts of the face consist of four main elements: the eyes, nose, mouth and ears. The following sections will study each of these components individually to help you to correctly represent their characteristics. It is advisable to study their structure and ways of representing them from different points of view.

THE IMPORTANCE OF THE EYES

The eyes are the most emotionally powerful part of the face since they transmit a vast number of expressions that reflect a wide variety of feelings. Of all the features the eyes, along with the lips, are the most important. The eye fits inside a spherical form that corresponds to the eye socket. Inside this shape are the eyelids, the upper one being slightly more almond-shaped than the lower, and the eyeball slightly hidden by both. The tear duct is in the inside corner of the eye, next to the nasal septum. Finally there are the eyelashes, which in women are longer, more curved and thicker than in men. The first drawings of eyes should be naturalistic, then, once the structure has been understood, you can begin attempting to stylize, enlarging the pupil, exaggerating the eyelashes and modifying their form to obtain a specific kind of expression.

The shape and arching of the eyebrows play an important role in the expression of the eyes.

The basic scheme of the eye is obtained by superimposing a circular shape on another, almond-shaped one. The eye seen in profile may be represented inside a triangular shape.

In the representation of the head in profile the drawing of the nose takes on a leading role.

In drawing fashion figures the facial features play a secondary role, and some designers even avoid representing the face at all. It is information that in many cases is irrelevant to the clothing that is the focus of the drawing.

When the figure is highly simplified the representation of the nose can be summed up in its minimal expression, in just two dots or a line.

NEED FOR A NOSE

The nose is the most prominent part of the face. In a front view it can be fitted inside a square or triangular shape, both elongated. Its representation is necessary when the face appears with exaggerated dimensions, with highly detailed features, as in a design for make-up. On the other hand, it is often highly simplified or even left out when the drawing of the figure is small in size or when stylizing is highly simplified.

THE BASIC DRAWING OF THE NOSE

To draw the classic nose shape, begin with the upper part, drawing a line that descends from the eyebrows to the tip. On reaching the lower part this line is interrupted and another is begun, drawing the wings of the nose by making two small curves (like brackets) on each side. The curve ends in a slight addition on both sides to represent the nostrils. The nose drawn in profile does not usually present difficulties. It fits best within a triangle; the right angle of the triangle is determined by the sides that mark the height and base.

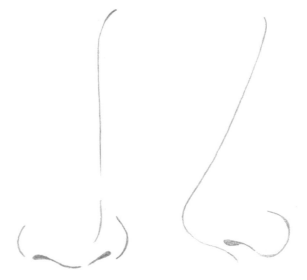

These two studies show, in a highly simplified way, the basic outline of a standard nose, seen from the front and in profile. All that is required is to pay attention to the form and direction of each stroke.

The mouth and ears

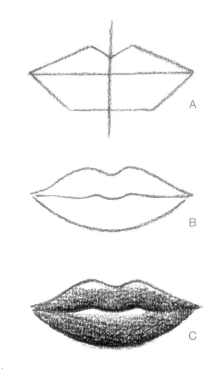

A

B

C

Despite appearances to the contrary, the mouth and ears are not very complicated to draw; they can be done with a few circles and lines. In the case of the mouth it is important to pay special attention to the undulating quality of the curves that form its outline, while the ears can be dealt with in a simplified manner and even left out, depending on the circumstances.

MOUTH

Symmetry is very important in many of the features of the face. To draw the mouth, a vertical line can be used as a sort of axis. On this line draw a horizontal straight line to form a cross, allowing you to establish the length of the lips. Then draw, gently, the outline of the upper lip, thin and elongated, which forms an arch just below the nose. Pay close attention to the slightly undulating line of the corner of the mouth, which forms a curving point. The gentle curve at the centre is important for establishing the shape of the upper lip over the lower. The fleshier and more prominent lip is the lower one, and the chin is drawn below it with a simple curve with almost no alteration. The mouth in profile does not present complications; it can be simplified with a triangular shape and is drawn following half of the outline above.

Here is a logical process for drawing the mouth. Begin by drawing the symmetry axes, in a cross, and then schematize the outline of the lips (A). Erase the previously drawn lines and over them redraw the outline of the lips, this time with more gentle curves (B). Finally, give them volume with a light shading effect (C).

The lips should look sinuous and fleshy, particularly if you are working on a line of make-up.

In profile the lips can be simplified as a triangle divided by a horizontal straight line (A). With straight lines make a outline of the shape of the mouth (B). Then erase the previous lines and on top of them draw others with a more curving, gentle line (C). Finish the mouth by shading, applying hardly any pressure on the pencil (D).

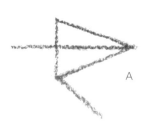

A

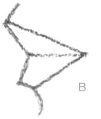

B

C

D

EARS

The ears are a part of the head that is very easy to draw, but, nonetheless, they are often poorly done. The outline is obtained with a very simple ellipse that is then modelled until the appropriate shape is obtained. Begin by making an outline with a circular shape. Inside it draw another similar shape that is smaller in size. From this initial outline finish constructing each ear. The internal folds are drawn with twisting, spiral shapes. Then the inside is lightly shaded with the pencil only slightly tilted. The ear cavity should not be shaded too dark or look like a hole.

STYLIZED, NOT CARICATURE

Every facial feature has a model of perfection, which was referred to earlier when studying the basic structure for drawing the eyes, nose, mouth and ears. Once you understand the naturalistic style of drawing, you can begin to focus your efforts on the process of stylization.

It is possible to modify the appearance or distort facial characteristics in such a way that, in spite of the distortion, those models are still clearly recognizable. However, you should avoid caricature or a comical characterization of the figure, since this is not appropriate for a fashion illustration. Stylistic variation should be limited to a style that brings out the beauty of the female or male figure and does not try to parody it or turn it into a cartoon.

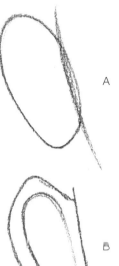

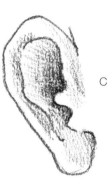

A

B

C

The drawing of the ear starts with an elliptical shape (A). A new circular shape is drawn inside. Notice that the treatment is highly subjective (B). The previous lines are erased and the outline of the ear is 'redrawn' to adapt it to the real shape and its internal projecting portions. To give it volume the drawing is finished with shading (C).

The mouth is made up of two moving parts: the upper lip, more curved and thinner; and the lower lip, larger and fleshier. It is a good idea to portray them differently in order to vary their appearance.

It is not enough to be able to draw ears in profile. Learn how to represent them from different points of view.

The ears are on a level with the nose, though this relationship can be dispensed with for the sake of stylization. Here the ear is represented as being smaller than the nose.

The texture of the hair is represented using more or less juxtaposed hatchings of strokes that follow the natural fall of the hairstyle.

The hairstyle should always be in accord with the design. Some stylists love to maximize the effect of their more classic creations by using elaborate hairstyles, to create an original and spectacular image.

Hair: textures and hairstyles

Hair and the way it moves is very important when drawing fashion figures, since the vitality and dynamism of the hairstyle serve to underline or complement the clothing. For haute-couture lines, classic, restrained styles are used. For street clothes, a more carefree line is more suitable; while for obviously modern trends, asymmetric and sculptural styles are in order.

TEXTURE OF THE HAIR

The hair is a malleable covering. It comes in a wide range of different forms and textures that represent a challenge to the beginner. The stroke should follow the logical direction of the hairstyle, so this should be taken into account every time the hair is drawn. In straight hairstyles the strokes are very straight, in wavy hair the lines are curved, curly hair is drawn with spirals and frizzy hair with a fine scribble. The tactile sensations of softness, smoothness and sponginess that hair suggests can be expressed with wash or by rubbing the strokes that have been made with pencil, chalk or pastel.

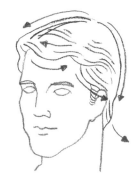

A hairstyle, however simple it might seem, can go in various directions. It is a good idea to pay attention to each of these directions in order to correctly represent the shape of the hair.

When the hairstyle is straight the strokes must also be straight. Similarly, if the hairstyle is energetic and voluptuous, the lines should express these characteristics.

It is a good idea to practise simplifying hairstyles. Summarize the shape and volume of the hair with a few strokes, leaving aside details and textures in search of stylization.

IMPORTANCE OF THE HAIRSTYLE

The hair and different types of hairstyles contribute, together with the other elements of clothing, to create the image of the model. So, just as the accessories are important, it is essential to finish off the figure with a suitable hairstyle that suits the style of the clothing, since it will make it clearer just what type of man or woman the design is aimed at. Hairstyles of various types will complement the philosophy behind the clothing and serves as a basis for personalizing different fashion trends.

DRAWING THE HAIR: FACTORS TO CONSIDER

To draw any hairstyle correctly, proceed in the following way. First the shape of the hair is drawn very simply, and the fall, curls or partings are sketched in. Then it is coloured in, bringing out the effects of light and shadow. Finally the texture is filled in, giving direction to the stroke and creating areas in which strokes are hinted at. The strokes help to express the fall of the hair or the direction of the hairstyle on each plane. The effect of smoothness is achieved by blurring or adding satiny highlights that give the hair a silky look. These effects are suitable if your drawing needs to be highly elaborate. In the case of a quick sketch the texture of the hair will hardly be worked on at all, but there will be simple shading consisting of straight, directional strokes.

Hairstyles, depending on their form, positioning and style, can give the head a modern or old-fashioned feeling, wild or demure, young or mature… It is a good idea to practise drawing different hairstyles to familiarize yourself with all the types.

1. It is a good idea to experiment with different techniques in dealing with hair. In this example ink and watercolour crayon are used. The first step is to draw the shape of the head with a pencil.

2. Moisten the paper with a brush, in the area that is going to be filled with the hairstyle. In this way the effect of the ink is limited solely to this area.

3. Try out a few brushstrokes with Indian ink on the moistened area. Observe how the colour spreads easily, creating different shades. Make some lines and strokes with a watercolour crayon on the patches of ink.

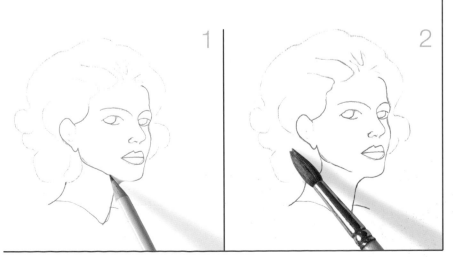

Studying the

ALEJANDRA BELMONTE
DRESS WITH ART DECO INSPIRATION, 2005
BLACK FELT-TIP PEN ON PAPER AND EMBOSSING IN BLACK

clothed figure

For the designer the clothed figure presents fewer initial problems than the nude figure, since clothing conceals the anatomical shapes and muscular profile of the figure. However, new challenges appear in the representation of garments: how to insinuate the volumes of the body through the clothing, how to reproduce the gestures and posture of the figure appropriately, the fall of the clothing and the folds and creases it creates. The key is in observing how the garment adapts itself to the contours of the body, in what is known as the 'hang' of the clothes. In other words, the fashion figure should act as a kind of hanger on which the clothing is displayed, without the anatomy taking on too important a role. It should facilitate a vision of the cut and the details of the garment, in accordance with the characteristics of the model.

Dressing the body, fitting the clothes

Though the outfit covers most of the figure's body (thus avoiding possible problems that may be inherent in drawing anatomy), with the clothed figure the problems have to do with the folds and pleats of the fabrics the clothes are made of, which require an understanding of the pose or the attitude the body takes on in specific situations.

FROM FLAT TO THREE-DIMENSIONAL CLOTHES

A flat drawing of a dress consists of a graphic, geometrically based representation that presents the garment as if it were on a flat surface or on a hanger. When this same garment adapts to the body of the figure, its folds and volume take on a more important role, the geometric outlines disappear entirely and are replaced by an irregular profile that is determined by the anatomy of the model. A drawing of a flat garment can be very useful, but when it is shown on the body, it is possible to distinguish with greater clarity its design and expressiveness.

The folds and shapes taken on by clothing as it covers the body hint at the anatomy of the figure. Depending on the type of garment, posture or movement of the figure is more or less perceptible. Bear in mind that the folds or creases usually coincide with areas where parts of the body bend (the armpits, knees or groin) and that some prominent parts of the body such as the breasts, elbows and knees are suggested by a gathering or stretching of the fabric.

The garment should adapt itself to the shape of the body and anatomy of the figure. A way of achieving this is to draw the clothing as if it were transparent.

With open, low-cut garments and those made from thin fabrics the form of the figure is more or less perceptible. A loose-fitting skirt facilitates the drawing of the pelvis.

The designs can be accompanied with drawings of flat garments (fashion flats) that look as if they were on hangers. It is not necessary to always draw the figure when presenting a garment.

THE HANG OF THE GARMENT

This depends on the fabric and the line of the garment, which gives the clothing a greater or lesser fullness, and has a lot to do with how it suggests the anatomy of the figure. It is easier to see the shape of the body under a silk dress or fluid jersey garment that clings to and shapes the body, than under a loose-fitting wool garment or a man's suit. So the way the clothes hang is established by the relationship between the length and the fullness of the garment and the area of movement between the fabric and the body. The more elastic a fabric is, the less it will hang. On the other hand, the looser and fuller a garment is, the more it will hang.

CARE WITH TIGHT CLOTHES

Tight clothing does not usually show creases and it reveals the anatomy perfectly by means of the outline, and because the form of the muscles can be inferred through the clothing. Tight-fitting garments do not hide defects in anatomy drawing: a hip that is too high, arms out of proportion or poorly drawn feet can be seen at once. This means that if you are drawing a figure with tight-fitting clothes you need to make sure you represent the anatomy of the figure accurately.

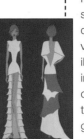

Representing the same figure from different points of view in the same illustration gives more information on the design and reinforces the impact of the garment.

The drawings on this page show how different clothes will hang on the same model. Tight clothes do not conceal the outline of the model's body; loose clothing conceals the anatomy of the body, presenting more folds and more of a fall.

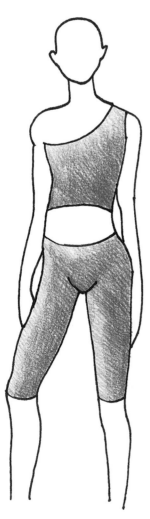

Any piece of fabric or article of clothing laid out casually over a table or chair will show many wrinkles and folds. This is an interesting subject for practice.

Folds and drapes

Drawings of clothing and fabrics of any sort represent an interesting challenge. It is important to take into account the fact that the drapes and folds of stylish clothing created by great designers are often very carefully studied and correspond to the character of the fabric, the direction of the fall and the articulation, movement and twisting of the body, which produces the folds in the garments.

PRACTISING DRAWING PIECES OF CLOTH

Draped and folded fabric can be seen as abstract subjects for drawing, given the geometric complication of the folds and the absence of any figurative forms. It is a useful exercise to practise drawing drapes and to work out the problems of drawing, chiaroscuro and modelling that occur. Do not worry about constructing the folds and their shadows too precisely; it is more interesting to interpret the drapes in an abbreviated, sketchy way.

Undulating folds are represented with an outline based on curved lines. Then the shading is done with gentle gradations, distinguishing each undulation of the fabric.

Fabrics in gathers present diagonal wrinkles that can be simplified with a vigorous zigzag. The shading is drawn in the inner part of each of the folds.

DRAPING A DRESS ON A TABLE

A good exercise for learning how to represent the folds and drapes in a garment consists of using pencil or charcoal to draw the folds and general shape of a dress that is hanging or laid out over a table or chair. The object of this exercise is to study the logic of the folds and to construct their volume combining linear strokes with a light shading effect in a uniform tone. The key is to correctly observe the way in which the cloth falls and to reduce each relief to a series of simple forms.

STIFFNESS OR SOFTNESS OF THE FOLD

The folds of the garments that wrap around your models may seem thick and rigid or subtle and filmy, allowing the viewer to make out the shape of the body they cover. The way a piece of cloth folds depends on the stiffness of the fabric it is made from. Practise representing the folds according to the fabric the garment is made from. If you learn to correctly represent this effect you can express in your designs not just the fall and the direction of the folds in a garment but also give information on the quality of the cloth. In other words, geometric, stiff folds with sharp edges indicate a rigid, starched fabric, while curving, flowing folds are typical of softer fabrics such as velvet.

The appearance of folds in a skirt is determined by the fall of the fabric. You must also take into account the direction marked by each fold.

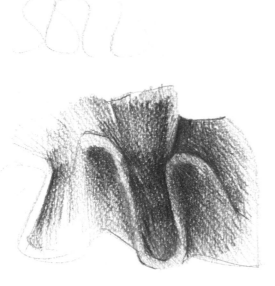

To give volume to folds, start with an outline in the form of an arabesque. The shadows are highly contrasted, which helps give plenty of relief to the garment.

Shading is used to create the effect of a bias is in a tubular form. To increase the look of relief, shade in gradations on each fold.

Falls, bias and creases

The drape is the form in which a fabric hangs (forming folds) on a body or another fabric. Many designers use all sorts of drapes to enhance their designs. Before learning to draw drapes it is a good idea to get to know them and distinguish the basic types.

FABRICS THAT ARE BEST SUITED FOR DRAPES

Any fabric can be draped, but the most suitable types of cloth are those that combine two basic features: they are thin yet have a fall and weight. The most frequently used fabrics are jerseys, gauzes and silks, though crepe, chiffon, georgette, fine satin or lace is also suitable. The same garment will fall in very different folds depending on the fabric from which it is made.

EACH FABRIC HAS ITS OWN FALL

In the mannequin illustration shown here the falls of two different fabrics can be seen, both being of silk that is light and transparent. The one with a large fall is silk gauze with big folds and a lot of movement. The other is a stiff organza with which it is possible to obtain big volumes, gathering or creating folds. Each fabric reacts in a different way to a bias, gather or fold, so it is important to be familiar with them before drawing them and to have a clear idea of their structure in order to include them in your pictorial repertoire, since each type of fold will be suitable for a specific design.

Using a mannequin as a support, hang different pieces of cloth on it in order to analyse them and draw their fall.

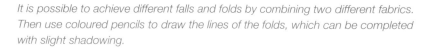

It is possible to achieve different falls and folds by combining two different fabrics. Then use coloured pencils to draw the lines of the folds, which can be completed with slight shadowing.

It is not enough to let a cloth fall freely. The designer should structure and create folds in order to draw them with linear strokes. To understand their direction and structure it is not necessary to use shading.

Gathering consists of running a thread through the cloth and pulling on it to form loops. The upper part of the cloth becomes contracted while the lower seems lighter, almost without volume.

DRAPING

Draping is the action of forming more or less ordered folds to give a creased texture. It is generally done with fine fabrics – silk gauze in this case – that create gentle, delicate folds. For practice find some fabric that has a good fall and can be gathered on a mannequin to create small, parallel folds. Then analyse its fall and folds and try to draw them with a linear stroke, without any shading. Note how all fabrics crease in different ways.

WITH AND AGAINST THE GRAIN

A fabric is made up of interwoven threads. To find out the direction of the thread you need to know the direction of the selvages, which correspond to the natural fall of the fabric, namely the direction of the principal threads of the weave of the cloth. The direction against the grain is that which is marked by the filaments that cross, on the perpendicular, the thread and form the weave. These two principles can be applied to all fabrics except felt (a fabric made from pressed wool) or a knit fabric.

The direction with the grain is the orientation of the main threads. Against the grain is perpendicular to this and is determined by the filaments that cross it. The bias is characterized by the diagonal of the fabric.

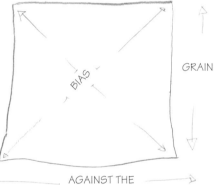

GRAIN

BIAS

AGAINST THE GRAIN

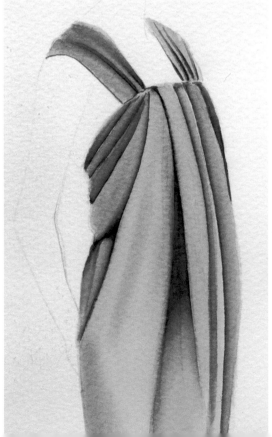

Once you have drawn the structure of the folds with linear strokes, the effect of volume is achieved by using shading. Here is an example of a highly elaborate garment.

In spite of the careful colouring, if you look closely you will see that the trick consists of developing slight gradations along each fold with a colour. The colour is lighter in the central part and darker as you get closer to the outer outline.

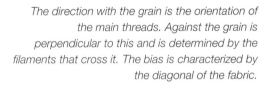

Looking at the two sketches you can see the difference between a fall with the grain (A) and another on the bias (B). In terms of drawing, the falls with the grain create folds with more emphatic lines and controlled shading. Folds on the bias can be drawn with more undulating lines, curves and more pronounced shallows. This means more contrasting shadows.

FALL ON THE BIAS

'On the bias' means cutting along a line diagonal to the selvage instead of a parallel line. This generally produces a movement and fall which is more graceful than that created by going with the grain. The longer the cloth is, the more extensive the natural fall, and in addition more waves and movement are added to the fall on the bias. With a stiff fabric the drape is less obvious.

PLEATS AND FLOUNCES

Pleats are pressed folds in the cloth that form a line running from top to bottom. The fabric is then folded over and set using heat. The pleats can be whatever size is required. Their width stops where the next pleat begins. A succession of vertical, straight, regular pleats is used to introduce details in both short and long skirts and dresses. Pleats come in a wide variety of designs. Among the most popular is the tiny 'Delphos' pleat, which imitates the folds of Greek tunics, and the 'sunray', which, as its name indicates, opens out like the rays of a sun, forming a fan. A section devoted to pleats and gathers cannot ignore the 'flounce', where the fabric is gathered to create fullness and volume.

Pleats tend to be used to give texture to the garment or to make it more beautiful. Given their simplicity, these are perhaps the easiest folds to draw.

Pleats are stiff and pressed and have a very structural look. They are represented by drawing straight and broken lines, forming a zigzag.

DRAWING FOLDS AND USING SHADING

When drawing and shading folds it is important for your pencil to respond to the sensations produced by the material the figure is wearing, in order to describe correctly the form of the folds so that they can be clearly recognizable in the design. The volume of the folds can be indicated by working on the shading, with contrasted shading for full volume or with gentle gradations to represent subtle folds with forms that stand out only slightly from the body. In both cases the shading appears in the inner part of the folds while the parts that project the most are presented as white, without any touching up.

Fix a piece of cloth to the mannequin with pins creating extensive, sharp and clearly defined folds. This simple model will be the subject of your next study.

The folds of a dress can be drawn with a good deal of simplification. It is enough to indicate the direction and contrasts between light and shaded areas, as is the case with this figure done in brush and ink.

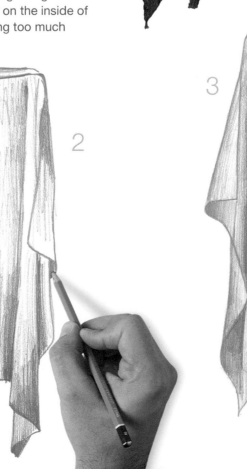

With brush, ink and a little water you can do a simple sketch to analyse the changes in tone.

1. In the following three steps, you will attempt to give volume to a linear representation of the drape on the mannequin, though in this case you do not need to take into account the fact that it is a black cloth.

2. Hold your pencil at a slight angle and extend your shading only on the inside of the folds and without using too much pressure.

3. To bring out the effect of volume, develop extensive gradations and contrast in the most shaded areas. Leave the light areas of the fold in a pale shade of grey.

Depicting textures

The type of fabric or tactile appearance of the material from which a garment is made can strengthen or ruin a design. For this reason it is advisable to learn to represent textures convincingly, to get to know the pictorial effects that can give your material a tactile look.

LEARNING TO SIMPLIFY TEXTURES

There are three basic ways of recreating the texture of a garment. The first consists of drawing, in a meticulous, almost scientific manner, the texture of the material, with its folds, creases and relief. The second, more preferable, alternative is based on observation and seeks to capture and represent a specific texture in a simple and informative way. This means distributing only a few relief effects over the garment, depending on the contrast provided by the light. It is a matter of suggesting the texture with small details, while the rest is filled in by the spectator's imagination. The third method is collage, not using pieces of paper but scraps of cloth.

USING SCRAPS OF CLOTH

Work with textures is not limited to drawing but can also include the incorporation of bits of material in sketches or designs. Many designers prefer to draw their inspiration from the texture and handling of a material rather than seeking to find the perfect form for a creation. This is a quick, direct way to represent the designer's needs, a way of looking for textures that help to make up the garment. In the investigation phase of a project you can experiment by gluing, stapling, sewing by hand or machine, making cutouts or adding appliqué.

When working with a garment made of angora or fur it is not necessary to shade in the entire surface in a meticulous fashion. It is perfectly acceptable to work up one area incompletely or to draw a furry or woolly outline.

When working in your sketchbook it is often not worthwhile wasting time trying to represent the textures of some materials, particularly if pieces of material and embroidery can be used in their place.

The textured appearance of many materials and accessories can represent an obstacle for a designer who is not very skilful at drawing.

EMBROIDERY

When you are drawing or painting an embroidered surface you need to examine the original material closely. You will normally be using linear instruments such as pencils and felt-tip pens rather than brushes for such a task. Representing embroidery, in spite of its apparent simplicity, involves paying attention to detail, manual skill and meticulous care in drawing the complex design of certain areas, and it is not a bad idea to have some knowledge of the basic skills required. Just as with other materials, if the embroidery is repetitive or the piece quite large, its representation can be simplified, leaving blank areas that are hinted at and not reproduced in detail.

FUR COATS

Fur garments are characterized by thick fur that is of varying length and overall they have a soft-looking surface. To paint them, first recreate the shape with colour, without putting too much stress on the direction of the brushstroke. Some shading or a wash of a light or medium tone is all that is required. Then, over a base of colour, the shape and texture of the fur is filled in with a rounded, fine brush, using a hatching of superimposed lines. This will be perceptible most of all in areas where dark colours coincide over light ones. In coats with short fur, the play of contrasts on the surface of the fur is what produces the sense of texture.

It is possible to directly capture the designs of some pieces of embroidery and reflect them on paper. All you need to do is to place a piece of tracing or lightweight paper on top of the embroidery and rub with a pencil. The pattern of the embroidery will be captured by the effect of the rubbing.

Embroidery requires more attention to detail. The drawing of the garment on the figure should be simplified but should be accompanied by samples or more detailed attached drawings.

Patterns and drawings of embroidery need to be done very carefully. For this reason the best instruments are linear: a pencil, a felt-tip pen or a pen with a nib.

1. Here the texture of a fur coat is represented in three simple steps. First draw the shape with a pencil and paint the inside with black wash.

2. With washes of brown mixed with grey represent the distribution of light, giving a greater intensity to the places where the shadow darkens the fur.

3. With the point of a round, fine brush, suggest the texture of the fur using fine, superimposed brushstrokes. Leave the lighter parts untouched, so the texture only appears in the shaded areas.

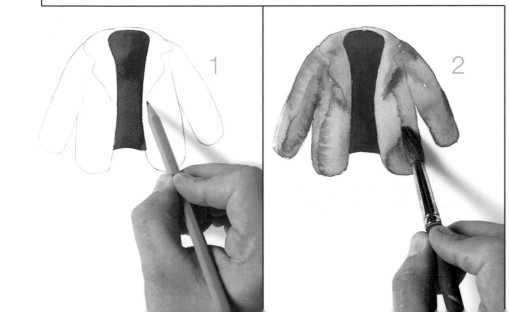

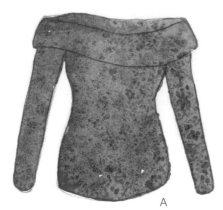

A

C

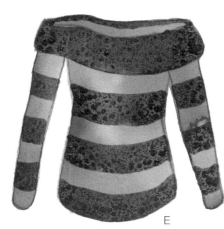

E

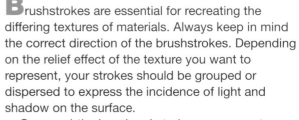

Creating textures with the brush

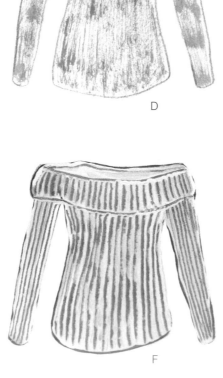

B

D

F

Brushstrokes are essential for recreating the differing textures of materials. Always keep in mind the correct direction of the brushstrokes. Depending on the relief effect of the texture you want to represent, your strokes should be grouped or dispersed to express the incidence of light and shadow on the surface.

Some subtly done brushstrokes can recreate some sensation of texture and volume in your painting. But if you work with watercolours, coloured inks or gouache you can achieve different textures by using a series of techniques and tricks that open up a range of possibilities to bring out further tactile qualities of the garment.

A. Granulated effect obtained by sprinkling grains of salt on a watercolour wash while it is still moist. Once it is dry, rub the paper to remove the salt.

B. First moisten the drawn garment with water. On the moist paper, paint with watercolour or acrylic. The paint spreads, creating blurred outlines.

C. With a white candle, rub the surface of the drawing of the garment. Then, using diluted acrylic or watercolour, paint on top of it, to obtain a marbled effect.

D. With a bristle paintbrush, using very little paint, make a dry, fluted, broken stroke to recreate the texture of a knitted garment.

E. On top of a green watercolour wash that is dry, dissolve a little sugar in a wash of the same colour. By using this method you will achieve a change of intensity and brightness.

F. Cover the drawing of the garment with a uniform violet. When it has dried, paint over the garment again, this time with beige acrylic. With the point of a cutter, cut lines through the still-moist colour.

SHADING THE TEXTURES

To give an impression of shading on a garment with a light texture, it is not necessary to completely cover it with a representation of the texture of the material. You can spread the texture effects in a controlled, premeditated way, with a contrasting treatment and with detailed strokes, ensuring that they coincide with the shaded parts of the texture and leave the lighter areas free and untouched.

TRANSPARENCY AND GLAZES

Transparency is the quality that lets light penetrate a material, so that the shape of the body behind it can be seen. Though this effect is known as transparency, actually materials are not totally transparent but translucent or semi-transparent. Tulle or net are just some of the fabrics that allow the form and tones of the object they cover to be made out, acting as a filter to modify the way they are perceived. When working with watercolours or acrylics, using glazes is the most appropriate way to create transparent effects.

FOLDS WITH TRANSPARENCY

A body that is behind a veil undergoes a process of distortion of colour and loss of definition. A veiled garment does not appear stiff and smooth but presents creases and folds, so that the transparency is modified by the superimposition of layers of material, a factor that complicates a drawing. When there is a fold the transparent effect is notably reduced, and if several folds are placed one on top of the other this effect disappears completely and the colour of the garment is intensified, though it appears with less light.

When shading a textured garment, the texture is frequently only represented in the shaded areas.

1. To illustrate transparency first draw the figure and paint the flesh colours without any clothing.

2. When the colours have dried superimpose on them highly transparent washes of colour. Use a first coat to silhouette the garment and a second only on the folds.

Each fold means superimposing a new wash on the underlying colour. Thus in the lighter areas there is only one wash, while in the darker ones three glazes of the same green are superimposed.

Patterns: exploring form and colour

Clothes often become an 'empty canvas', a surface on which to let graphic skills, fantastic figures and colours and unusual designs in the form of patterns run free. As a fashion designer you need to appropriate some illustration techniques in order to represent your patterns.

EXPLORING NEW DESIGNS
Making a print means experimenting with shapes, colour effects and graphics. This is a highly creative working process. You can take some paper, prepare a palette with a variety of colours (gouache, inks, acrylics or watercolours) and pick up the brushes to give your imagination free rein, combining polka dots, swirls and scribbles to decorate your favourite fabrics.

REPETITION OF A DESIGN
Repetition is the repeated use of elements of design, details or adornments in a garment. A brief note of colour or a very simple interplay of spots can be used as a pattern that is repeated until it completely covers the surface of the design. These designs, composed of striking shapes and colours, are the basis for making patterns for continuous fabrics that are then printed using either transparencies or photographic film.

It is a good idea to experiment with different colour effects, strokes, patches of solid colour and graphics on paper or cardboard. Some of these colour notes may become the pattern of your next garment.

All you need is a design with a strong graphic effect that can be used as a pattern for continuous fabric.

To obtain original patterns you can resort to your traditional paint box and experiment with creative mixtures of colours.

OVERSIZING AS A WAY TO SEE THE PATTERN

When representing patterns on a figure, designers usually present only the part of the body that the garment covers or the entire figure with a size that is larger than usual, in other words oversized. The patterned garment can be shown in a larger size or in a box that makes it possible to distinguish the print better and to see how the design adapts to the body.

SHADING PATTERNS

To mark the shadings on a patterned garment you have two options. The first consists of showing the maximum detail of the pattern of the garment in the areas where the shading is evident. The patterned drawing seems less detailed and even blurred in areas that receive direct light. The second option is based on differentiating the light and shade on a pattern by painting the shaded zones with more intense and saturated colours and the lighter areas with lighter, softer colours. In this way one single colour can present variations of tone depending on the part of the garment.

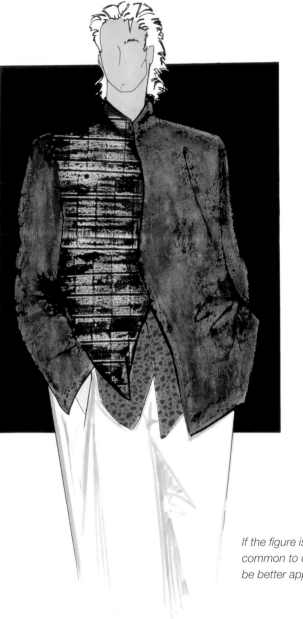

A sketchbook can provide an interesting tool area for drawing patterns. On it you can set down ideas, colours and shapes that will help you to complete the style of a garment.

If the figure is wearing patterned clothing it is common to oversize the shirt so that the design can be better appreciated.

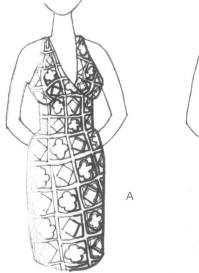

A

B

If you wish to shade a pattern only with lines, make the stroke stronger in the shaded areas. In the lighter parts the drawing will look more diffuse (A). If you are working with colours, the tones of the parts in shadow will be more saturated and intense, while the lit side will present paler colours (B).

CONTRAST AND HARMONY IN PATTERN

Contrast and harmony are two basic principles of the design of patterns, given the major role of colour in the designs. The effect of contrast of bright, saturated colours calls attention to the garment and breaks the monotony of the whole. On the other hand, harmonic contrasts imply similarity rather than difference, thanks to a combination of colours that do not clash and materials that combine well. If you are going to make a subtle pattern without much contrast, you need to slightly exaggerate the contrast between the colours in your illustration to prevent the slight nuances from being easily lost.

PATTERNS THAT CAN MODIFY THE PERCEPTION OF THE FIGURE

When applied to the different garments in the wardrobe, some patterns create optical illusions that modify the look of the figure who wears them.

Patterns can be hard or soft, and suggest stiffness or flexibility. For example, a print shirt with superimposed organic or geometric shapes in bright colours completely conceals the anatomical features and gives a dynamic appearance. Patterned skirts or dresses with horizontal, diagonal or vertical stripes modify our perceptions of the body's silhouette, making a person look fatter, thinner, taller or shorter. Patterns can be used to emphasize or conceal physical characteristics.

Working with saturated and opposing colours of the spectrum gives very striking patterns.

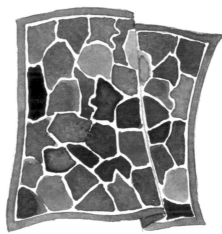

If you require a more harmonious effect you should work with colours of the same range, such as blues, for example.

Patterns do not just add a note of colour to models but can also modify the silhouette and the characteristics of the figure.

STRIPES

Stripes can modify our perceptions of a figure. They can lead the spectator's glance across the garment, up and down, sweeping diagonally or in a zigzag ascending the body. Here are the most common types:

- Vertical stripes emphasize height and make the figure more elegant and slim, because they move the glance up and down the body.
- Horizontal stripes focus attention on width, making the figure look shorter and stockier.
- Diagonal stripes give the fabric a dynamic effect.
- Striped patterns can also be divergent: the stripes can run in opposite directions.
- Curved stripes give a garment more femininity and can be used to reduce the shape of the waist or to lead the spectator's glance to the body's curves, breasts and hips.
- Radiating stripes emerge from a single point as if they were rays of light. This pattern is often used in the design of skirts.

A

B

C

D

E

A. Vertical stripes make the figure look slimmer.
B. Horizontal stripes make the body seem wider.
C. Stripes on the bias give the garment a dynamic effect.
D. Diverging stripes create tension.
E. Patterns with curved stripes modify the appearance of the body's silhouette.

The pattern does not always have to be repeated in a regular fashion. An apparently arbitrary distribution makes a pattern more expressive and gives the garment greater spontaneity.

Checks never go out of fashion and can bring elegance to a garment.

Basic shading of the figure

In fashion drawing shading is not very extensively used. However, it can be appropriate when it helps the shape of a garment to be seen more clearly, since contrasts of light and shade enhance the effects of volume, textures and contours.

THE DIRECTION OF THE LIGHT

The best light to work with to illuminate your figure is light that falls laterally, preferably from a slightly elevated position. This ensures that the light on the figure illuminates one side and leaves the other side in shadow. This contrast allows the contours and folds of the garment to be clearly represented and the volume of the figure is enhanced. This marked contrast of light and shade is essential if you wish to emphasize the volume of, or the creases in, a garment. Pencil shading on a figure should be applied with flat, solid tones, using a block shading technique.

WHERE THE SHADING SHOULD APPEAR

It will now be clear which is the best option for illuminating a figure, but how should you put this into practice with a garment? How and where should you represent the shading? The areas that should be shaded are those where the material is folded over on the body, such as collars, the inner

Shading with a thick line is symbolic and stylized. It is used to emphasize one side of the body with a thick stroke done with a marker.

line of a jacket and pockets; zones that are slightly raised or that show a definite hollow or sinking, such as necklines or folds at the armpits; and those that stand out due to a marked effect of volume, such as under folds and on the inside of arms, sides or legs.

Shading appears on the side of the figure opposite the point of origin of the light.

When shading a garment it is important to pay attention to the direction of the light, the folds of the material and projecting parts, such as pockets, lapels and collars.

USING A THICK LINE

A method that is frequently used by fashion designers consists of bringing attention to one side of the figure with a thick line, generally drawn in with a marker pen. A fine stroke is associated with the illuminated area, whereas the thick, intense stroke, with which the opposite side of the body is drawn, opposite the light source, is interpreted as a representation of shading. This shading method gives an initial sensation of relief and depth to the figure, as well as emphasizing the outline of the body.

DETAILED SHADING

In finished illustrations for a project shading is not usually simply sketched in nor is it based on extensive, roughly drawn patches. Work will be done more meticulously in order to recreate the texture and folds of the garment accurately. This need not be a complicated operation. All you need to do is to take two or three colours that are similar, though of different intensity, and combine them to form gradations. Coloured pencils used with a moist brush are particularly suitable for this, since they are delicate, with gentle but dramatically effective tones and are ideal for fine, detailed finishing touches.

Special attention needs to be paid to the creases on the sleeves and at the joints of the body. Students often neglect these areas.

1

2

3

4

1. To fill in the shading on a pink dress with watercolour coloured pencils draw the silhouette of the figure and then mark the creases with a red pencil.

2. With a pink coloured pencil paint the entire surface of the dress with gentle strokes.

3. On top of the pink strokes darken the shadows of each crease in the dress with magenta. The illuminated areas are left pink.

4. To finish unifying the strokes and smoothing the shading go over the colours with a moist brush.

Techniques for shading garments

Before shading a garment you need to study with the way the light falls on the garment, decide what style you wish to express through your illustration and what features and aspects of the garment you want to emphasize. Once you have made all these decisions you can choose the shading that will best suit your needs.

LINEAR SHADING

When you are shading with linear instruments such as pencils or felt-tip pens, first draw the outline of the garment. Then the most prominent folds are drawn in a very simplified fashion. The fold is always drawn starting from the inside out, never the other way round. Then the interior of each fold is darkened by making a hatching of diagonal strokes that may appear juxtaposed or superimposed on one another. Note that this way of working with hatching is quite adequate for the sketching phase, but is not so suitable for more highly elaborate projects, for which shading should be done using wash.

1. This example shows how shading is done using hatching. The starting point is to create a figure with the pencil.

2. Hold the pencil at about the middle and hatch lines to mark in general shading. Use very little pressure.

3. Intensify the shading by superimposing more hatching on top of the initial lines. Hold the pencil closer to its point to apply more pressure.

4. Two or three layers of hatching, at the most, are sufficient to correctly shade a figure using linear strokes.

COMBINING LINES AND WASHES

A combination of lines and washes is the most complete method of creating shadow and the one that is usually the best choice for fashion design. The procedure consists of doing the entire drawing of the figure and its clothing using lines, first clearly marking the outline of the garment and its creases and folds, and some indication of texture and then finishing with a wash of highly diluted black ink to provide shading.

This is, of course, if you are working only with monochrome tones. The wash can also be done with different-coloured watercolours.

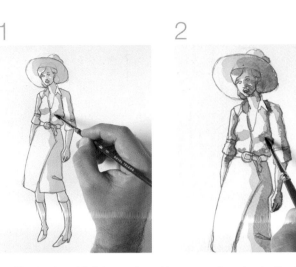

1. To shade with ink washes, the procedure is similar to that described opposite. Paint the shaded side of the body with blue paint diluted with water.

2. Over this wash, when it is dry, apply a second coat that is more intense and that contrasts with the shading.

3. With only two tones of blue you can obtain a simplified but effective representation of the fashion figure.

Gradated shading is suitable for simple, not very detailed figures.

Realistic or classical shading is the best for representing relief and the textures and creases or folds of the garment.

Symbolic shading is purely decorative. It does not have any descriptive function or provide any information on textures or folds.

THREE TYPES OF SHADING

In fashion illustration the shading techniques are classified into three basic types.

- Gradated shading, used on garments that show creases and folds and are represented using a general gradation. The aim of this shading is simply to give a feeling of volume to the figure, without dealing with details or textures.
- Realistic or classical shading, used for garments that require a high level of detail, since it is related to the academic, detailed drawing that is capable of describing textures, folds and creases meticulously. Sometimes this shading tends towards a treatment that is close to the pictorial language of the comic.
- Decorative or symbolic shading, as its name suggests, is purely for decoration. It merely gives an impression of shading as part of the overall composition of the design.

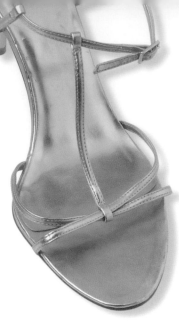

Drawing accessories

Accessories represent a bodily extension of the garment, a way for the creativity of the design to be extended to the neck, hands, head or feet. Fashion accessories are becoming more and more important in the wardrobe, which means that the designer has to take them into account and exploit their potential for complementing a garment.

Shoes are a key element in any woman's wardrobe; they can make or break an outfit.

ACCESSORIES AS SYMBOLS

As objects whose original function was utilitarian (belts, hats, handbags) or one that was initially magical (jewels, bracelets and necklaces), accessories have come to take on a markedly ornamental function; they have begun to acquire the status of authentic artistic creations. Accessories have turned into symbols that serve to differentiate and personalize, the ideal complement for clothing, distinguishing those who wear it from the rest, making it a symbol of individuality and authority.

CREATIVE WORK

The fashion designer must be sensitive to and interested in learning about and interpreting the trends and aesthetic lines of each season's accessories, in order to select those that are most suitable for the clothes he or she is designing and those that will best enhance the quality of the garment, its balance and also its commercial potential. It would be a good idea to acquire some knowledge of the techniques and determining aspects of footwear, handbags, jewellery, hats and other accessories in order to use them to complete your collections. They can offer a world of ornament and touches of the romantic, of exaggeration or of the exotic, whichever is appropriate to your style.

Jewellery fulfils an ornamental function. Many clothing firms design their own accessories.

When designing shoes it is useful to have the artistic skills needed to represent the texture of the materials.

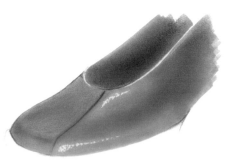

SHOES AND HANDBAGS

The effect created by shoes is determined largely by the shape of the sole and the heel. In addition to adding to the height of the woman wearing them, high heels are often used to increase erotic attraction, draw attention to the legs and set off clothing more elegantly. Something similar occurs with handbags, which often match the garment, sharing colours, shape and texture. Most designers create unique pieces, taking their inspiration from graphic arts or from the customers' preferences. Extravagance, opulence and originality all contribute towards women's shoes and bags in the twenty-first century, while men's shoes seem to have remained more conventional in terms of design. Sports shoes, however, have undergone a terrific evolution, and there is, it would seem, an infinite number of designs.

HATS

In addition to protecting the top of the head from inclement weather, the hat has long been used as a symbol of social distinction and political or ideological orientation. Nonetheless, it was not until the twentieth century that it was democratized and acquired a decorative function. Women have worn hats in a multitude of shapes, colours and materials, while men have almost always worn them in their most traditional forms. A discreet hat can give the final touch to the correct line of a style, particularly for women, when it really helps to individualize a garment. Nowadays the traditional hat often takes second place to different sorts of caps, but, regardless of the shape and the material used, any way of covering the hair is a sign of allegiance to the fashion of each period, reflecting its dominant values and tendencies.

In the world of fashion illustration shoes tend to be drawn with a very high, sometimes exaggerated heel.

A hat can provide a touch of originality and personalize any outfit.

When designing accessories the drawing should be much more precise and explicit than for fashion figures. Here is an example done with a permanent felt-tip pen.

Using the drawing as your base, the colours and texture of the leather of the bag and the metal of the frame are represented using gouache and pencils.

Developing a
project

Knowing the customer

ESPIGA / TWEED

BERTA SESÉ
TEXTURES PROJECT, 2000. FELT-TIP PENS AND COLOURED
PENCILS WITH FABRIC SAMPLES.

and the market

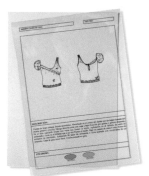

The objective of fashion is to come up with attractive products that adapt easily to customers' needs. This means that the designer has to investigate and interpret fashion trends and develop their creative and technical capacity, adapting their own ideas to the needs of the market and the demands of the fashion industry. It is not enough to come up with original proposals or to be a torrent of creativity. A designer must try to establish a degree of empathy with the consumer and produce work that is commercially viable.

Customers and companies

The world of fashion does not just focus on the garment as a product of artistic creation. It must also be seen as an industrial product that can be adapted to the varying needs of the market for wide distribution. The designer has to take the trouble to get to know potential customers and adapt to the preferences of different consumers and brands.

STUDYING THE POTENTIAL CUSTOMER
Before beginning a project it is a good idea to study the potential customer's needs. Your objective is to try to imagine a profile of the customer that is in tune with your designs and with your concept of clothing. When sketching the psychological profile of the customer take into account their sex, age, economic status, profession and any other factor that might influence a fashion choice. If you analyse each of these aspects and try to find answers to these questions you will be able to draw up a profile that comes quite close to your potential customer. Given that the designer's objective consists of satisfying the customer's needs, always from his or her own personal point of view and style, your study should have an influence on all aspects of

the design, including the choice of fabric and colour, the formal or informal character of the garments and, of course, their likely final cost.

ANALYSING THE MARKET
Trend studies enable the designer to predict the intentions of the possible customer. In preparing these analyses various general factors relating to demography, sociology and economy have to be taken into account. Knowing such information beforehand is very useful to a designer.

Trend studies analyse the purchaser's habits according to age and population distribution (it is obvious that a greater demographic concentration means a larger number of potential customers; on the other hand, people dress differently in a small town than in a city or on the coast). How people live and work is also studied, along with how these factors influence the way they dress. People dress according to their social class and purchasing power and like to identify themselves with that status. These studies, along with those provided by commercial fashion establishments (which analyse the behaviour and preferences of their customers), all have to be carefully considered in order to predict important trends.

People dress differently depending on their geographical location. Urban fashion is more daring and brighter colours tend to be worn.

Study your potential customer. Your sketchbook is a good place to collect photos, ideas and designs that make it possible to analyse the market in order to decide on the style best suited to your project.

THE STYLE OF A FASHION HOUSE

Many designers are connected with fashion houses that invest a great deal of their money, time and experience in developing new fashions or innovations. When these achieve acceptance and become successful, the fashion house then protects its product and gives it a unique, easily recognizable identity. At this point the designer often has to sacrifice his or her personal popularity to work anonymously for the benefit of a group that is committed to the style of the fashion house. All famous brands have their own particular style that is reflected in their design philosophy. The designer as an individual loses importance and what really counts is the presence in the media of the fashion house and the link that the public makes with the style of clothing it represents.

THE IMPORTANCE OF STYLE

Style is something above and beyond seasonal fashion. The identification of a fashion house or brand with a clearly defined, specific style is fundamental to its success. Its designers must work for the good of the brand, keeping any individual traits to a minimum, with the common goal of creating a style, an attitude that expresses a way of thinking, living, dressing and acting. The style of a fashion house or brand should be related to its perceived profile of the customer and should find a way to establish a connection with a group that has interests and a lifestyle similar to those expressed by the design of the clothes. This connection is achieved when the clothing is in tune with the customer's personality, creating a sense of harmony between the customer's inner personality and outer appearance.

In the studio of a large fashion house the designer works anonymously, adapting his or her creativity to the style of the brand.

When working for a brand of shirts, even though the brand has a definite style, the designer can still include individualized features. Designs by Divinas Palabras, 'the TV or not TV' collection.

CREATIVE LIMITS

When considering working for a fashion brand, a designer faces certain limitations that should be understood and evaluated before deciding whether or not to work for a particular company. The designer has to find the proper balance between being faithful to his or her own tastes and pleasing the customers, particularly if the fashion brand has a highly defined style that limits creativity. It is important to become accustomed to being objective and to try to be self-critical, looking at designs from the point of view of the company executives who are going to have to give them their approval. A good design and the design that most attracts you as a designer are not necessarily the same.

THE CONCEPT OF THE BRAND

The brand comes first, while the designers and creators of fashion remain anonymous. In a brand the styles of the creations are subordinated to a corporate image, a specific characteristic, a logo, a signature, an accessory or particular aspect of the design that identifies the manufacturer. The emphasis is on brand recognition, as is making clear the garment's connection with the style of the fashion house to which the garment belongs. A customer selects one brand or another because he or she identifies with the style of dressing, the attitude it expresses, the lifestyle with which the product is associated, or because he or she wishes to attain that attitude with the help of the product.

You will be asked to create garments that are not entirely in accord with your own style or taste. The genuine professional is valued for their capacity to put enthusiasm and passion into designs for a different taste than their own.

When you work for a big fashion company you must find a balance between your own taste and what the brand is asking for. Here are some sketches of designs for sweaters for a commercial firm.

The design of a garment for a big fashion company involves a process similar to the one outlined in this book. The difference is that the company is involved in the design from the beginning, from the first sketch.

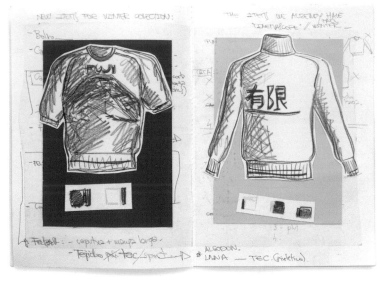

In fashion schools the future designer is not just trained in how to create an original design but also in pattern design, printing etc.

Many fashion firms take an interest in designing accessories for their collections. So it is a good idea to practise drawing accessories frequently and to note down the features and individual aspects of each design.

PLANNING A FASHION LINE

To introduce designs onto the fashion market the first step is to create a 'line' in the commercial sense of the term. Planning a line involves considering the novelty and modern character of the garments, conceiving designs in terms of a complete wardrobe of clothing that presents a common, unified concept, with a balanced set of pieces that go from top to bottom: clothes that can be combined in many different ways, can coordinate and are interchangeable, even, if necessary, with pieces from other brands or another designer. The objective is versatility, to tempt customers to buy the largest possible number of clothes. Exclusiveness is aimed at a segment of the public that is much more limited in size but with a higher level of purchasing power.

The exclusive designs that appear in fashion shows are not aimed at the general public. These fashion-show customers have a high level of purchasing power.

In a big fashion company the designer tends not to participate in the work of pattern design. In a small fashion house, on the other hand, the designer is usually involved in making up the prototype.

The collection: a group of ideas

Once you have determined the type of company or customer you are going to work for, the style that interests you is decided and the research process is finished, you now have a story to tell. This is the moment to get to grips with designing a collection. Once the process is complete you should find reflected in your designs your source of inspiration, the theme or link that brings the project together and its objectives.

CREATING A STORY

Before you can begin to design a collection it is essential to find a theme, to develop a line of garments based on a single source of inspiration, with a design, a range of colours and textures that are consistent with the collection, and that link it to your story or concept. You can note down some themes or ideas and then select the best and arrange them according to stylistic affinities and evaluate the possibilities for creation, originality and versatility that each one offers. A good exercise consists of making a photo collage that brings together images that are relevant to the theme selected, to serve as a source of inspiration and at the same time become a way to connect and relate your ideas together.

DRAWING SKETCHES

Once the theme is clear, a large number of notes will be taken and quick sketches will be drawn, almost without thinking (brainstorming). The idea is to get your first impressions of the subject down on your sketch pads, draw figures and designs in series and accompany them with written notes that contain further information that might be useful. Then, work with the ideas, draw and expand on them, try different variations on the shapes, colours and materials you have chosen, perhaps experiment with new shapes for sleeves, necklines etc. It is important to learn to think laterally, compare impressions, evaluate ideas and feel comfortable about talking out loud about your ideas.

The process of documentation is fundamental to finding a subject for your collection. You will find inspiration in the works of the great fashion couturiers.

Starting from a principal theme, different interpretations and adaptations of garments are drawn that are interrelated through a line, a style and certain adornments or details.

The sketching phase helps to clarify the line of the collection. The next step is to get some models in colour down in your sketchbook. The design and structure of the drawing should now be quite clear.

When you come up with a good idea try to get all you can out of it. This is a matter of thinking of multiple variations on the idea, in this case a patterned hat.

THE OBJECTIVE IS CONSISTENCY

To create a collection it is necessary to develop a wide range of related ideas in order to produce clothing that functions not just as individual outfits but that is also consistent as a group. This means that the garments should have a variety of forms and uses and an aesthetic relationship and, whenever feasible, it should be possible to combine them. Focusing systematically on important factors such as style, colour, cut, shape, use of similar patterns and production all contributes to giving a collection consistency. The selection of materials and samples can begin when you are satisfied with the designs and think it is worth developing a pattern for them.

GUIDELINES FOR CREATING A COLLECTION

To summarize, when you are creating a collection you need to consider the following points:

1. Determine the number of outfits that are going to be designed and work out how many garments each outfit is going to consist of.
2. Brainstorm. Get down on paper all the ideas that occur to you for developing the collection: shapes, cuts, accessories. Everything is useful.
3. As the concepts come together and the designs become clear, a list of garments should be made to avoid repetition. They can be divided into tops/shirts, dresses/trousers and jackets.
4. Create one or more silhouettes to determine whether this is a collection for daytime, nighttime, party or mixed.
5. Establish a chart for materials and colours.
6. Finally, the finishing touches are defined: clasps, trimmings, prints, embroidery…

The collections should be composed of versatile garments that can be interchanged and combined. In other words, the top on one figure can be combined perfectly with the skirt or trousers on another.

Developing a collection

The theme of the collection is related to the clothing of the ranchers of the American West.

The following section will review the principal concepts on which a collection is built. A real project will be studied, together with the steps taken by a professional designer; you will see how the designer sticks to a concept and to the unity of aesthetic parameters, and how the choice of colours, prints and materials contributes to give the collection consistency and unity.

THE THEME OF A COLLECTION

Once the phase of sketches and drafts is finished, the main objective is to create a collection that is consistent with the theme. In this case the story of the project is related to the aesthetic of the American West, the world of ranches and cowboys, full of jeans, checked materials, knotted neckerchiefs and wide-brimmed hats.

To give the collection its own identity, the designer needs to study the theme in depth in order to communicate the concept in a clear and simple way. Messages of colour, shape and texture that are well-defined and clearly related with the aesthetic of the American rodeo are more effective if they are free of any gimmicks, adornments and illustrations with irrelevant characteristics.

In any collection there should be two points of view: one that is general, that shows a consistency with the whole, and another that is individual, since each garment should have a unique universe and be created in detail, so that people will fall in love with it.

A selection of representative elements such as jeans, wide-brimmed hats, neckerchiefs, dungarees and jackets are sketched in pencil.

A CONTENTS SHEET

One way to plan a line is by making a series of sketches of all the outfits, to show the whole collection together, as a unity. They can be drawn in a series in succession, in a very schematic and sketchy way, on a piece of paper, like a table of contents of all the outfits. This way of planning the collection makes it possible to ensure the unity of the collection, study the effect of the silhouettes of the garments, check that no design is out of place and, in short, get the most out of each form.

PIECES THAT CAN BE COORDINATED AND INTERCHANGED

The design of a collection can be reinforced with the compilation of a range of colours and strong patterns and a series of prints, in this case blues and checks. The construction and finishing of each piece needs to be well thought out in order to ensure the maximum number of possibilities in the cowboy line have been shown.
The designs in the collection should have substance and include important, fundamental ideas and less spectacular pieces. But be careful. Though the collection should offer a rich variety of well-coordinated and interchangeable garments, make sure you avoid unnecessary duplication.

The selection of the most representative materials in the collection needs to be kept in mind. In this case checks best suit the theme.

The contents sheet shows all the models that make up the collection in a schematic, simplistic fashion.

The final step in the project is to illustrate the definitive designs, including the details. The representation of the garment should be absolutely clear.

Finding
sources of

ÁNGEL FERNÁNDEZ
TWO FIGURES WITH FABRIC SAMPLES, 2003.
COLOURED PENCILS, ACRYLICS AND COLLAGE.

inspiration

In the search for inspiration, the expert designer is constantly investigating, keeping his or her eyes open to channels of information about the world of fashion (magazines, innovations from the competition, new fabrics), assimilating subtle aesthetic changes and, above all, observing people. The designer should pay attention to changing times, be open to new ideas and scrutinize his or her immediate surroundings in search of themes or motifs that could be incorporated into new designs. The designer should also keep informed of the appearance of new materials, printing techniques, buttons, fasteners or any other materials related to fashion design.

Clippings provide valuable information and offer sources of inspiration for the clothes you design.

Gathering information

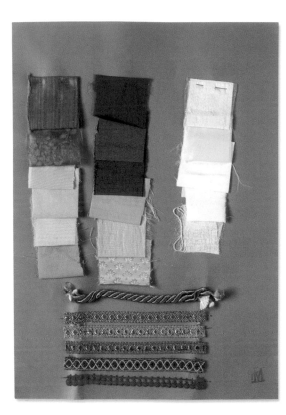

An index of materials.

Magazines, fashion publications and trade fair catalogues keep design and styling professionals in touch with the great couturiers and with the principal centres of creativity in the world (Paris, London, New York, Milan etc.). Try to keep new trends and what is really new in design within your reach, take it all in and note down what interests you most in an album or your sketchbook.

MAGAZINES

Fashion and style magazines are a constant source of inspiration, brimming with numerous photos of the latest creations, the most stylish models and poses for drawing. They are a way of keeping in contact with the latest trends and most recent additions to the world of fashion. As a designer you need to become a collector of images and articles of interest, useful visual information on the clothing you like, ingenious designs and solutions or original collections.

And don't just turn to today's fashion magazines; you can also find inspiration in old magazines, second-hand books or even old family photos. Make photocopies when you cannot tear out a page from a book that is valuable or belongs to a library.

COLLECTING INFORMATION AT FAIRS

If you have the opportunity to travel, there are design competitions, fashion shows, fairs and commercial events for materials and fabrics all over the world. Any of these events will take you to the sources of the fashion industry, gathering first-hand information on innovations in colour and forecasts, types of fibres and fabrics, new lines of clothing for men and women etc., all of which will help point you in the same direction as the best professionals in the sector. Many stylists continually travel throughout the world, collecting information to publicize in fashion magazines or provide to the firms and brands in the sector.

Visiting furriers or textile fairs is a good way to make direct contact with the materials and put together a collection of samples that can be numbered and arranged on pieces of cardboard.

Be inspired by photos of your favourite designers' garments, transforming them and adapting them to your own style.

EMULATING YOUR FAVOURITE DESIGNERS

Clippings from photos, magazines, journals or fashion show programmes should be kept in your sketchbooks. When this information is mixed in with your own sketches, notes and drawings, it makes it possible to combine visual information with your own inspiration and your impressions in the form of drawings. You can also gather visual information on your favourite designers and try out sketches inspired by their creations. Avoid blatant copying of course, but start out with someone else's design, modifying it slightly and incorporating different finishes or textures, trying to give the project your own style. You have to strike a balance between stylistic 'plagiarism' and originality.

SKETCHBOOKS AS SOURCEBOOKS

Sketchbooks should be used regularly, along with the camera. They form a personal archive of resources for everything you find inspiring and stimulating, a kind of visual diary that collects any interesting idea or garment worthy of inspiration. They should be sourcebooks where you collect photos of people, body postures and clothes, pieces of fabric, colour charts, everyday objects and decorative shapes that you have cut out and pasted in carefully. The idea is to put together, on a double page spread, different items that will help you to develop your own thoughts. Once you have brought together enough images and ideas, you can begin to develop your designs.

With the passage of time these sketchbooks can become a useful archive to turn to in order to derive new inspiration or recover ideas.

Use your sketchbooks as sourcebooks. Paste in photos, clippings or fabric samples, grouping together ideas that may be useful at some point.

The shape of objects

A simple paper lampshade is the object of study here. Its androgynous shape leads to the following design.

Design schools encourage students to draw aspects of real life, to study the environment, the milieu in which students live, and to try to see objects as an inexhaustible source of ideas. The results become more surprising as you progress further and further away from the original object towards new creative channels.

A PAPER LAMPSHADE

If you observe what is around you with the eyes of a designer you will see that inspiration can be found in any place, object or concept which you can make into your raw material. A simple paper lampshade can suggest the idea of a dress. Its delicacy and fragile and sinuous form attract the attention. On the basis of a close observation of the object you can really appreciate what you find inspiring or beautiful: the silhouette, the way the light illuminates the paper, the interior framework of ribs that hold it together and maintain its volume.

LINE STUDIES

The object is placed, well lit, in the centre of a table and line studies are made. In the sketchbook various interpretations of the object are drawn, in an attempt to analyse it and to internalize its shape and the principal lines that define it.

Getting to know the object better is the first step towards capturing its essence and discovering which shapes and peculiarities to maintain and which ones to discard when the lamp is turned into a dress.

These drawings can be done in pencil. A few lines, reinforced with light shading, are enough to give the object a sense of volume.

1

1. The purpose of the first drawings is to assimilate the form of the object, sketching variations with different interpretations in a sketchbook.

2. Check the fit of the design by adapting the shape of the object to a figure. A number of variations are studied in order to discover the best alternative.

2

DRAWING 'DOLLS'

The next step consists of adapting the form of the object to the body of the figure. Spontaneous sketches of 'dolls' are drawn that are then dressed with garments inspired by the shape of the lamp. Here it is a matter of studying the degree of fit that the silhouette offers. Figures are drawn in front view and in profile, and are dressed with different interpretations of the model. It is not enough simply to repeat the same version on different 'dolls'. Change some aspect in each version so that each sketch seems different from the previous one. The result is a broad spectrum of models that will help in choosing the definitive design.

THE LAMP DRESS

Finally, the design that will enable the lamp to be transformed into a dress is chosen, and a more detailed illustration is made. The outline of the figure is drawn on brown paper with a white pencil, showing the silhouette and the definitive approach to the design. The flesh tones of the figure are painted with pink gouache and black is used for the hair. Then the dress is covered with white gouache. When the paint has dried, an ochre coloured pencil is used to draw the structural lines of the dress over the layer of paint. Brown paper is chosen as a background for this design because it contrasts well with the white of the dress.

3. Next, a slightly more definitive figure is drawn. On brown-coloured paper the shape is outlined with white pencil.

4. A touch of colour is provided by black and pink gouache in the hair and flesh tones and white for the dress.

5. With an ochre coloured pencil the structural lines on the white of the dress are drawn. The finishing is very simple, without frills.

6. After the design phase the lamp dress is made. Here is the result of this project, by Irene Villaseca.

A tissue-paper pompom

Inspiration can be found in any object, or any minor detail. Its form, texture or colour can act as a lure, attracting your attention, becoming the fruit of your analysis and turning into the origins of a new garment that is striking and original. An example of how this process takes place is described below, starting from a simple tissue-paper pompom.

GEOMETRY IN PAPER

The object in question is a decorative tissue-paper pompom. When opened up it presents an interesting geometric shape, a 'beehive' made up of flexible and extendible rhomboid 'cells'. It draws the viewer's attention to the folds of the paper, the play of light and shadow, the geometric hatching, the lightness of the object in spite of the volume it represents, how complex and yet how simple it is at the same time.

The source of inspiration for this design is a decorative tissue-paper pompom.

One of the origami pompoms was pasted on the silhouette of a fashion figure in order to study the possibilities of the garment..

This figure shows the definitive design, with the adaptation of the pompom to a skirt shape.

The finished project, by designer Gory de Palma.

It is useful to have various samples of the same pompom. This makes it possible to study it carefully, paste it onto figures, or take it apart to study how the folds are joined and glued together.

The piece of tissue paper is transformed into a skirt of nylon tulle that has the same accordion folds as the original pompom.

ASSIMILATING THE OBJECT'S CHARACTERISTICS

The idea is to incorporate the system of folds of the pompom into a new design that assimilates the object's characteristics: a play of contrasts that allows for a great deal of volume, modifies the silhouette of the figure with a great lightness and combines the complexity of the interplay of lines with a very simple construction.

The first step was to make a sketch on a piece of black cardboard. With a graphite pencil the silhouette of a figure was drawn and then filled in with white gouache. When the paint was dry a white tissue-paper pompom was pasted onto the drawing, giving the appearance of a folding skirt.

THE DEFINITIVE FORM

The next step is to finish defining the rest of the dress. A more elaborate figure was drawn with the distinct appearance of the dress. Some changes were made to the form of the skirt. The hems form a shape like an inverted pointed arch. At the same time, the number of cells that make up the beehive-shaped structure was reduced. The next step was to find a suitable material for the skirt. It needed to be simultaneously stiff and light in order to recreate the cellular structure of the pompom. All that was then left to do was to prepare the patterns and construct the dress. The result of all this work is to be seen in the dress itself, designed by Gory de Palma.

Inspiration from architecture, history and art

The boundaries between design, architecture and the plastic arts have become more and more blurred. Today almost all the artistic disciplines have moved closer together due to a common denominator: creativity. Many artists work closely with fashion designers, and designers, in turn, work with musicians, industrial designers, illustrators, interior decorators and architects. It seems that the lines separating the different artistic disciplines are beginning to dissolve.

THE STRUCTURAL NATURE OF OBJECTS

Geometry is the basis of all forms. Thanks to the geometric structure of objects and architecture, they become the focus of attention of the designer who is eager to confront new challenges. Their shapes are studied, simplified and adapted to the body to offer new ways to interpret the silhouette. Such garments are daring creations that stand out because of their sense of volume. Such themes are very tempting for any student of fashion design, but they have limited commercial possibilities.

This design was inspired by the dresses of the eighteenth-century royal courts, with ruffs, a cropped jacket and heavy embroidery. Project by designer Lola Cuello.

Architecture is a source of inspiration for the most daring designs.

Architecture as an inspiration for the fashion designer is justified because of its structural and geometric character. It is particularly appropriate if you want to design garments with plenty of volume.

LOOKING FOR THEMES IN OLD PAINTINGS

Another important source of inspiration for the fashion designer is to study and analyse the details and cut of clothing from different historical periods as seen in paintings and engravings. A careful observation of the silhouettes, textures and forms of the clothing of the past will help you to discover new combinations of ideas and materials that will satisfy your curiosity as a creative designer.

DECONSTRUCTING CLOTHES FROM THE PAST

Here are two projects inspired by fashion from the past. The first, pictured opposite, takes its inspiration from the court dress of the seventeenth century, characterized by ruffs, puffed sleeves, voluminous skirts and heavy embroidery. The second project takes as its point of reference the costume of nineteenth-century England with its wide skirts and elaborate coiffures. In these examples, though they bring together some of the historical characteristics of mannerism and the Victorian period, the garments have a totally modern appearance thanks to the process of 'deconstruction'. This process involves dismembering the piece and isolating its characteristic features in order to study them individually. Then they are brought back together and combined with modern features to achieve a contemporary design carefully balancing the old and the new.

1

2

1. Many dresses of the Victorian period have been reproduced in antique engravings. Dresses such as these can inspire many modern creations.

2. After studying the engravings ideas are structured and the design is clarified. The design options are then drawn in the sketchbook.

3

3. Once the process of creation is finished, the final design looks like this, a Victorian-inspired dress reconstructed to look more modern. Project by Anna Vila.

Studying the silhouette

A number of silhouettes drawn in a very stylized fashion are shown on a single page. Several can be drawn, with the goal of showing the volumes most commonly used by modern designers.

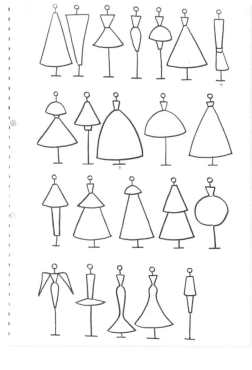

The silhouette determines the drawing of the exterior of the garment, altering the outline of the figure. The viability of dresses with a large silhouette is related to the female form that is considered to be the ideal of each period, and to the designer's capacity to create an attractive silhouette with light materials so that the dress does not weigh too much.

THE FORM OF THE DRESS

The line is the silhouette of the dress. It corresponds to the volume and the length of the dress in relation to the body. This is the first impression of a garment, the general form it offers when viewed from a distance and before details are noticed. The cut of the dress is one of the elements that give form to the silhouette, along with other details such as the seams, the quality of the fabric and ornamental finishing touches that push the material outwards. These elements increase the perception of the volume of the garment and they include high collars, fringing, flounces, folds, shoulder pads or fancy decorated sleeves.

THE LINE OF THE BODY

The design of seams, folds and openings can also modify the perceptions of the silhouette of a dress, since these elements create an emphatic visual effect. For example, if the material is tight below the breasts or a blouse is fastened crossways

When drawing a figure that emphasizes the silhouette of the dress, exaggerate it with a great deal of stylization. Look at these examples from a sketchbook.

These drawings show how the cut has an influence on the proportions of the dress. The same silhouette has three distinct variations.

the torso should be stylized, reducing the volume of the silhouette at this point. If, on the other hand, necklines are eliminated and the blouse's collar is made higher, the neck is shortened and attention is centred on the face. This section examines some of the possibilities for modifying the silhouette of shirts, blouses and short dresses. For example, if you are looking for a visual balance between the parts of the body you should tighten the waistline to divide the silhouette into an upper and lower part, providing a harmonious effect.

GAINING VOLUME WITHOUT GAINING WEIGHT

When working with garments that have a lot of body, do not make the mistake of thinking only about the impression the dress is going to make from a front view. Garments with a good deal of volume often need to be planned in their entirety, considering all the angles and the effect the outline will have from all 360 degrees. The viability of silhouettes with a greater volume is determined by the qualities of the material with which the dress is made. Tulle or padding can be used or the dress can rest on a constructed frame to increase its volume without having too much effect on its weight. Dresses with a big silhouette represent a big challenge for designers.

SILHOUETTES AND THEIR VARIATIONS

Down the ages silhouettes have changed to adapt to the tastes of the time. However, the forms or volumes most frequently used can be grouped into a few generic types generally represented by simple geometric forms that, superimposed on the figure, simplify the appearance of the dress. Numerous variations evolve from these basic models, depending on the preferences and trends of the moment.

The drawing opposite shows on a single page some models that have been constructed with a very simple geometric design with the main objective of emphasizing volume and line. Making templates with paper dolls like those represented here can be very useful for considering the silhouette of dresses when working on a collection. Bear in mind that a collection should not have too many variations in silhouette or it will diminish the general impact of the collection and thus weaken the message.

Changing the openings and seams on a dress can help to stylize or loosen up the silhouette. Here are some of the most common types of dresses.

Fabric as a source of inspiration

Material is an important source of inspiration and a stimulus to creativity for the designer. Study the behaviour of fabrics and materials, look at degrees of softness and textures and experiment with a mannequin or by dressing a model. Remember that the fabric you select will affect the construction of your designs.

FABRIC AS RAW MATERIAL

Many designers sketch their ideas on a piece of paper, but others prefer to work directly with the material, handling the fabric. A good way of studying the real behaviour of a fabric is to wrap it around a tailor's dummy or to analyse the behaviour of the material on the body when it is used in a garment. Sometimes, after completing a design some of the materials you had in mind (types of fabrics, linings, buttons etc.) cannot be found on the market. If you work for a large company this will not be a problem because all the elements can be manufactured according to your needs. A small fashion house or an individual designer, however, has to make do with what is available. For that reason it is much easier to buy your materials first and let them speak to you.

The mannequin is the designer's inseparable companion. It is the most patient of models, a natural hanger on which to study the behaviour of fabrics.

Folds, falls and creases that different materials make can be the inspiration for your next creations. So always make drawings of concepts that might seem useful.

CONSISTENCY OF THE FABRIC

The behaviour of the material on the figure depends on its consistency, stiffness, handling, transparency, softness, fluidity and tendency to wrinkle. Soft materials, for instance, have a lot of fall, and adapt well to the body's silhouette. In addition they can be crossed at the waist or neck. If the material has a stiffer or more complex structure it seems to expand, takes on volume and modifies the exterior profile of the body. In these cases a simple silhouette should always be maintained in order to avoid a confusing general effect. It is important to be aware of the structural nature of the different materials, understand how each fabric responds in certain conditions and always make your designs with all these characteristics in mind. It is necessary to accumulate a basic knowledge of the different categories of fabrics and their suitability for different uses. A material cannot be forced into a style or form that is not compatible with its practical or visual characteristics.

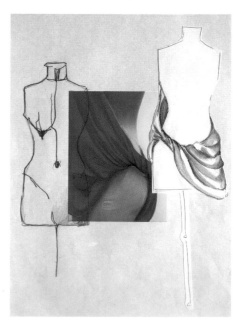

TACTILE FABRICS

A garment is not just something visual. It is also a sensory experience that should stimulate the sense of touch. When a fabric is chosen for use in designing a collection it is not just its visual properties that are taken into account, but also the feel of it. Clothing should also be touched. Some garments transmit sensuality and delicacy through touch – silk or cashmere, for example – while others give a sense of hardness and strength to an outfit, as with leather or heavy denim. It is the skilful contrast of textures that makes the play of sensations more intense and the garment or outfit more attractive. Learning to successfully combine the different tactile qualities of the fabrics is a valuable skill for every designer.

COMBINING DIFFERENT FABRICS

A garment can sometimes combine two or three different fabrics. This is more likely when you are designing an entire collection, and it can present problems if you are not organized. In such cases, avoid using too many colours and materials, otherwise the collection will seem diffuse and lacking in coherence. On the other hand, if you use too few materials you run the risk of being boring and coming up with models that repeat themselves. Success, as always, is to be found in balance, in working with a suitable number of different fabrics, and in choosing three or four principal fabrics, which will be given more prominence, and designing other secondary materials for finishing touches, adornments or minor details.

To better control the effect of the fabrics in your collections, as you are drawing figures put in references or samples of cloth next to the illustrations or sketches.

When gathering scraps and samples of fabrics you will find that your own preferences and style are revealed in your selection. Your choice of materials will project your image and identity.

Touch and feel fabrics, study their texture, their colour and their brightness under different light conditions. Remember you can stimulate the sense of touch through the eyes.

Modelling folds

Modelling is the process through which compositions with folds are made on the mannequin with toile or sheer muslin before using other fabrics which have more body or which provide greater volume. This is a very important exercise for every designer and it is usually accompanied by drawings of the results of the garments modelled on the mannequin.

A WAY OF WORKING ON YOUR IDEAS

Modelling can be used as an instrument in the search for ideas, allowing for immediate, rapid and effective contact with the material. The general rhythm of the work is transformed into a finished idea, into a garment prepared and modelled, forming folds. This is usually done with inexpensive cotton cloth to avoid wasting more expensive fabrics. Once the modelling is complete, the work is usually complemented with drawings. Various sketches are made from two or three different points of view by just walking around the dummy. The drawings allow analysis of the positioning of the folds in a way that is clearer and simpler than would be the case with a photograph. In addition, drawings can be accompanied with notes in the margin providing useful information about how the garment is to be made.

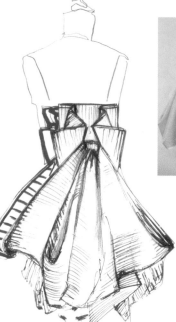

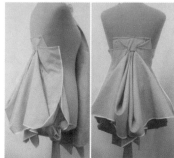

Modelling with the material on a dummy can be a good drawing exercise that can be dealt with by sketching and with a variety of techniques. It is a good way to learn to draw folds and to master shading.

Every idea you try out on the mannequin should be represented by a minimum of two drawings. Make sure you vary the point of view.

MODELLING A PART OF THE BODY

When modelling with fabric, you can concentrate on just one part of the body. For example, work can be done on a shoulder, the neck, the breast, a hip or whatever part of the body most inspires you. The exercise consists of modelling just one area of the mannequin, creating part of the garment with the material at hand. The rest is completed with drawing, inventing and interpreting what the drapes should be like and trying out variations in sketches. This is ideal practice for helping you understand how the material adapts itself to the body and its fall. Here the adjustment of the garment (with its loose parts and seams) becomes very important.

DRAWING WITH FABRIC SAMPLES

Each drawing of the mannequin should be accompanied by a sample of the fabric used for the modelling and also of the material you plan to use to make the dress. This will give your designs a certain quality since the fabrics chosen for modelling are often cheap. If you happen to have information about the fabric's composition, width, price and point of origin you can note this information next to the sample. Any personal observations made while working with the material should also be noted down next to the drawing. This shows a sensitivity and interest in the material selected.

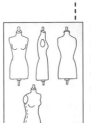

For drawing it is useful to have first prepared a template of the mannequin that you can trace or photocopy.

It is not necessary to model a whole garment. A detail is sufficient; the rest can be drawn on the final pattern design.

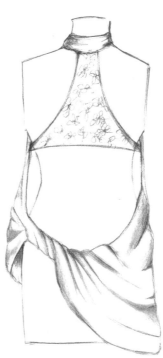

To accompany the drawings of the modelling, two scraps of material are pasted to each page with the material selected for the actual garment.

Exploring collage

As a designer it is essential to explore all the techniques of illustration that are available. Collage is a good option for stimulating creativity, freeing you temporarily from more conventional drawing techniques and enlarging your visual vocabulary.

AN EXERCISE IN SIMPLIFICATION

Cutting and pasting pieces of paper of different textures and colours on a paper is a reflective exercise, and it requires an effort to learn to simplify the garments of the model in a few cutout shapes of coloured cardboard or art paper or from magazines. This technique involves combining ideas and visual elements that result in a satisfactory composition, and also makes it possible to reflect on and interpret the way the human figure is perceived and even to recreate surprising textural effects.

DRAWING WITH CUTTINGS

First sketch the form of the figure in pencil. Take two or three magazines and scan through them, looking for photographs with colours, textures or tonal effects that attract your attention. From the images chosen cut out the outline of the garments, making sure they are in proportion with the figure you have drawn. The outfits are created by pasting superimposed layers of different pieces of paper on the drawing. The touches of light can be represented with light-coloured paper and the shadows with dark paper. It is not necessary to always cut the pieces of paper with scissors; they can also be torn out to achieve more irregular outlines. You will discover that it is possible to dress the figure effectively without having to worry about correctly reproducing the silhouette of the dress or its actual proportions.

Collage is seldom presented alone. It is usually combined with other graphic alternatives such as acrylic or gouache.

Different colours and textures with which to prepare collages can be taken from fashion magazines.

Collage is a good way to incorporate colours, forms and textures into your own figures.

Collage can be used to beautify your designs. Here the cloth has been cut to silhouette the figure and at the same time to provide information about the material of the garment.

It is sufficient to draw the form of the figure using a fine line and complete the form, colour and texture of the dress and the hat with cuttings from a magazine.

COMBINING COLLAGE WITH GRAPHIC EFFECTS

Compositions done with collage are very useful for capturing an impression, as an exercise in simplification and to experiment with the relations that are established between areas of colour. However, if you wish to obtain maximum performance from your fashion illustrations, aim to finish off the figure with some more precise and dramatic pictorial touches. It is not possible to reproduce exactly the details and finishing touches of a dress solely by cutting out pieces of paper. Collage can resolve the questions of the general structure of the design and its simpler aspects, while the profiles, fasteners, seams or texture effects can be left to the expertise of the brush. The most suitable paints are those that are opaque, such as gouache and acrylic.

COLLAGE OF MATERIALS

Scraps of material that you keep in your workshop, studio or at the bottom of your cupboard are an excellent source of raw material for collage. The working process is similar to using paper. However, you need to work with a brush and use white latex or paper glue. The drying time is much longer, but the final effect is striking. If you work with cloth of different textures and volumes you will be able to give your work an interesting relief effect that appeals to the sense of touch.

Collages with scraps of different types of material appeal to the sense of touch. Few people can resist the temptation to touch them.

The sketchbook: a laboratory of ideas

The notebook or sketchbook should become an essential instrument for the fashion designer. It is the best tool for inspiring, for stimulating your inventive capacity, collecting important information and developing ideas.

A COMPILER OF IDEAS

The sketchbook is a notebook for jotting down, analysing and developing ideas to use in current or future projects. It is also a testing ground, the place where clothing takes shape, and a personal archive in which to store up ideas that you have absorbed, such as clothing you have seen in museums, at fashion shows or in the street. It is a way of anticipating a theme or putting together factors that have attracted your attention.

AN ALBUM OF THINGS

Your sketchbook should be a folder that is capable of holding numerous cuttings, samples, fabrics, embroidery and other elements within its pages. Anything can be included if it brings something new and interesting to your ideas. It also works as a photo album in which to keep your first wardrobe tests, which can be some private photographs, maybe done at home with the help of a friend who acts as the model. This is a way to visualize your creations before making them public.

A sketchbook is a hotchpotch. You can keep anything in it that attracts your attention, even physical objects like photographs and scraps of cloth or samples of furs of different colours.

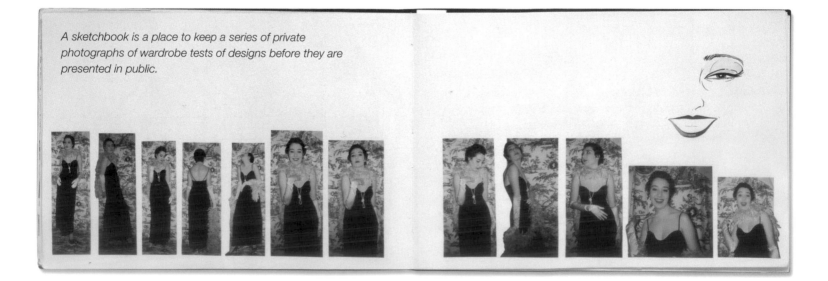

A sketchbook is a place to keep a series of private photographs of wardrobe tests of designs before they are presented in public.

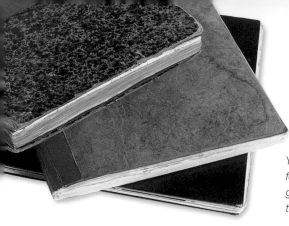

You should have various sketchbooks of different formats and sizes. They are the best tools for gathering ideas, analysing them and incorporating them in your creations.

This is a page from a sketchbook full of ideas and sketches one on top of the other in complete disorder. Drawings are quick and spontaneous.

Get your most important ideas down on paper by doing roughs of designs in a special sketch pad that you keep for this purpose. If you do not have one, you can use any notebook.

SKETCHED DRAWINGS

The drawings in a sketchbook are not very elaborate; they do not even need to be well done. Since their chief objective is to communicate or capture an idea, they do not pretend to be quality illustrations. The purpose of these sketches is to rough out a line, a silhouette or a formal characteristic and to capture indications of styles or colour in an abbreviated form. So most of these drawings are done very quickly, which gives a spontaneity and freshness to the stroke.

NOTES ON THE MARGINS OF THE DRAWINGS

In order to help you remember and be able to better process what you have observed, you can use notes on the margin of each drawing to provide information about colours and textures and the introduction of tonal values or colours. These notes are necessary when the rapid pace of events (as in fashion shows, plays, observation of people in the street) prevents you getting down everything you want in the form of a drawing. The sketches are thus accompanied by phrases, written notes that bring out important details, subjective impressions, dates, locations, indications of colour, ideas that have emerged on observing the subject, additional aspects etc.

On a double page compositions can be made with photographs of some of your designs. This is a good way of reflecting on the finished work.

Colour and

ANGEL FERNÁNDEZ
COLOUR SAMPLES FOR A COLLECTION, 2003
INDIAN INK ON PAPER

style

The game of seduction and persuasion in the world of fashion is directly related to the designer's use of colour. When drawing clothing for a collection you need to keep in mind the range of colours that is going to be used, a decision that should be taken while designing. This choice determines the power of attraction of the garment, the time of the year a line is linked to, and helps to relate it with a season. Some colours go out of style from one season to the next. To work with them with conviction you need to have some basic notions of colour and to understand the different possibilities of mixtures and the standard colour charts most often used in fashion and fabrics.

Understanding colours

In order to identify and classify colours you need to understand how they are distributed and respond, and how they complement one another depending on their position on the colour wheel. This knowledge is fundamental to being able to accentuate the character of the clothing you design according to your needs.

PRIMARY AND SECONDARY COLOURS

The colour wheel is a colour diagram that is based on the three primary colours: magenta, yellow and cyan (blue). They are defined as primary because they cannot be obtained by combining other colours. This means that the primary colours are totally autonomous and do not have a chromatic similarity with any other colour. If the primary colours are mixed with one another three new colours, orange, green and purple, are obtained, and these are called secondary colours. Positioned across from one another on the colour wheel, the colours are seen to be noticeably different and are called complementary.

RANGES OF COLOUR

Various mixtures of primary and secondary colours can be made. The new colours created extend the colour wheel, forming ranges and groups of colours formed by their similarity or chromatic proximity. It is important to take into account these ranges in order to limit the colours that are included in a collection and ensure that all the colour elements are combined in an orderly fashion. A limited range guarantees the natural continuity of the designs. As a general rule, the designs of fashion students should be moderate, avoiding the use of too many colours and using ranges of no more than eight. Using more colours does not mean that you improve a piece. Also, the more colours that are included in a range the more difficult it is to use.

The primary colours are magenta, yellow and cyan (blue). All other colours are derived from these.

Primary colours can be mixed with each other to obtain secondary colours: orange, green and purple. The mixture is demonstrated best using translucent fabrics.

Ranges are composed of one colour in different grades of tone and intensity. Here is a range of browns.

HARMONY AND CONTRAST

One way to achieve harmony is to use an analogous colour scheme: in other words, various colours that are next to one another on the colour wheel. A broad use of analogous colours can include three or four tones that are next to each other, with different degrees of brightness. On the other hand, if you want to emphasize or trim the shape of a dress you should choose two colours that are far apart on the colour wheel. It can be very effective to create forms by contrasting warm and cool, light and dark, or bright and dull colours. A strong contrast can be obtained between different layers of clothing.

STANDARDIZED COLOURS

There are two international codes for colour imitation recognized throughout the fashion industry, which avoid any confusion that might occur about the exact shade of colour required for a garment or to specify a tone. The colour charts most frequently used in fashion and textiles are the professional Pantone system and the SCOTDIC (Standard Color of Textile Dictionaire Internationale de la Couleur) code. Both are based on the method for measuring colour according to tone, value and intensity, the Pantone chart being the most popular. The system is made up from 1,900 colours, chromatically arranged by colour family, each with individual reference numbers. Pantone also has a specific equivalence chart for the colour of fabrics called TheRightColor.

Bright, saturated and contrasting colours contribute to defining the profile of a garment.

Analogous colours are found close to one another on the colour wheel. They do not clash and can be harmoniously combined.

Charts for colours and fabrics are usually accompanied by a manufacturer's reference number. This makes it possible to make the garment in the colour that has been chosen without any possibility of error.

Interaction between colours

Colours and tones should never be considered in isolation but on the basis of their relations with the others around them. Each new touch of colour that is added to a group alters the relationship between the colours already present.

SEASONAL COLOURS
Changes of season and climate are determining factors for choosing the colours to use in your collections. In autumn and winter people feel attracted to warm, cheerful tones or to dark colours that help to retain body heat. On the other hand, white, which repels the heat of the sun, and softer colours, of the pastel type, are used more frequently in spring and summer. Some colours come into fashion during one season and then go out of style. The ranges of colours that are popular change every season, except for black and white, which are timeless.
As a designer you should keep informed about the colour trends that are expected for each season. This information can be picked up by

visiting trade fairs, style websites and specialist magazines.

CONTRASTING COMPLEMENTARY COLOURS
Colours change the way they look depending on the context and the colours that are near them. A muted colour, because of the influence of the colours around it, can seem brighter. In the same way, a strong colour can be softened if it is accompanied by saturated colours. When two complementary colours of equal value are positioned together they cause a chromatic vibration that exceeds their true intensity, in what is also known as simultaneous contrast. When various complementary or saturated colours are positioned together forming stripes or patterns they cause a striking visual sensation. Because of the contrast, the colours seem more intense and compete to attract attention. In the areas of friction between the different chromatic zones a type of blinking sensation or 'vibration' is produced.

Stripes of contrasting colours – those that lie opposite one another on the colour wheel – are used in this garment, producing an active optical effect called a flashing contrast.

Every social situation and each change of season requires the appropriate colours. Here is a collection of party dresses in lively, saturated tones.

Complementary colours such as red and green produce a maximum contrast, and the colours seem more vivid and intense.

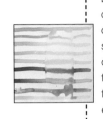

Before colouring a drawing, test the colours on a blank sheet of paper to check that they work together properly. A few brushstrokes are enough.

In a sketchbook the designer compares different ranges and tones that will help decide the final colours for the dress.

ADD A TOUCH OF COLOUR

When a range of colours produces harmony, it is sometimes common to introduce a counterpoint or 'touch' of colour, to form a slight but striking contrast that attracts the eye to this point and enriches the overall effect. Adding a surprising touch of colour in an unexpected tone can give the design a spectacular note. A chromatic difference can be tonal, a bright, light colour, a contrast of complementary colours or the opposition of warm and cool tones.

USING SAMPLES

To choose the definitive colour for your designs you can use colour samples of real materials. This can give you a more precise idea of how the colours will combine in the garment. This way of working helps you see what the best combinations are and consider what proportion of each colour there will be in the whole design. It is advisable to have clear ideas about this point since varying the proportion and combination of the colours can give a very different look to the same design. Combinations that work well in a range of colours can be spoiled if the proportions between the colours have not been worked out properly.

A counterpoint is where a highly contrasted colour note is added that brightens up the range of colours around it, as occurs here with the red.

Colouring techniques

Samples of pieces of material of differing chromatic values, with different degrees of intensity of a single colour.

The colours you use should be precise. They should not be mixed too much; they should be clean and not too unusual. It is important to have a wide range of colours in any medium you are working in. This way you can minimize mixing and reduce to a minimum any alteration of the original colours.

TONE, VALUE AND INTENSITY

There are three important concepts that must be understood and used correctly when dealing with colour: tone, value and intensity. Tone is an attribute of colour that is equivalent to the degree of displacement of that colour towards the neighbouring colour. For example, a yellow can have a greenish or orangey tone. Value is the transition from light to dark of a specific colour. It refers to each degree of variation a colour can undergo before turning into white or black. Finally, intensity refers to vividness. This is the degree of saturation or purity of colour. Diluting a pigment with water, for example, reduces its intensity.

MIXING COLOURS

Before preparing a range of colours it is a good idea to analyse how to mix them correctly.

• To reduce the saturation of a colour there are two basic methods: dilute the colour with water so that it thins and loses chromatic strength or mix the colour with white. White lightens the colour and also lessens its vividness.
• If you want to lighten a colour without making it lose saturation, use lighter colours of the same range. For example, to lighten brown use ochre, and to lighten ochre use yellow. White is always used as a last resort, since whitening takes intensity away from the colour.
• If you want to darken a colour without its losing vividness, proceed as in the previous case, but using darker colours of the same range.
• Avoid using black to darken colours. Black dirties other colours, making them cloudy and greyish.

It is best to avoid the use of black to darken a colour since it makes the result muddy. Instead, use darker colours that belong to the same range as the colour.

If you want to lighten a medium green use a yellowish green. To darken it use blue. Thus you can lighten and darken a colour while avoiding the use of white or black.

Two ways of lightening a colour: adding white (A) or diluting it with water (B).

HALFTONES AND MUTED COLOURS

Different ranges of colours also have emotional components. Halftones bring to mind the range of pastel colours. They transmit a gentle, light chromatic stimulation that brings delicacy to the colour and a refined, discreet elegance. They are obtained by whitening colours with strokes of dry pastels or with the wash effects of watercolours or gouache. Dull colours remind us of mineral substances or different materials that are found in nature, since they retain the shadows and pigments of the earth. They are very elegant. They are often appropriate for expressing severity in uniforms and suits.

IRIDESCENT AND MORDANT COLOURS

The diaphanous brightness of iridescent colours makes whites, beige, ivory, pinks or light, crystal clear greys shine. This is a demanding range of colours that enhances the qualities of materials such as silk or ivory. Mordant colours are intense and stimulating and full of vitality and dynamism. They become points of energy, an incandescent burning sheen of saturated colours.

To lighten a brown mix it with ochre and to lighten ochre add yellow. If you use lighter colours of the same range to lighten the colour you preserve its saturation.

A. The range of halftone colours recalls pastel tones.
B. Muted colours are the result of a mixture of a colour with brown or grey.
C. Luminous colours recall noble materials such as silk or ivory. They give off a sensation of light.
D. Mordant colours are more saturated, lively and cheerful.

Harmony charts bring together the different colours that make up a collection and that appear arranged in horizontal stripes. The proportion of each colour is indicative of the relevance it is going to have. Your first colour charts can be painted with brushes, but definitive ones can be created on a computer with the aid of a Pantone colour chart.

Styles of illustration

In fashion illustration it is important to choose the most suitable style in order to ensure that the work is presented in the best possible manner.

CHOOSING THE STYLE THAT SUITS THE PROJECT

There is no reason why you should remain faithful to a single style in the same way as an artist, sculptor or musician does. You should choose the type of illustration that matches the objective of your project. The illustration style selected should transmit the designer's original inspiration while at the same time reinforcing the ideas of the design, without affecting the presentation of the garments.

As a designer, your fashion drawings should be versatile and capable of change depending on the needs of the customer you are addressing.

NATURALISTIC STYLE

The illustrations shown here are in the naturalistic style, with a line that maintains a clear connection with realistic or academic representation. Here the degree of distortion of the figures is scarcely perceptible and carefully considered, and the figures show proportions that are consistent.

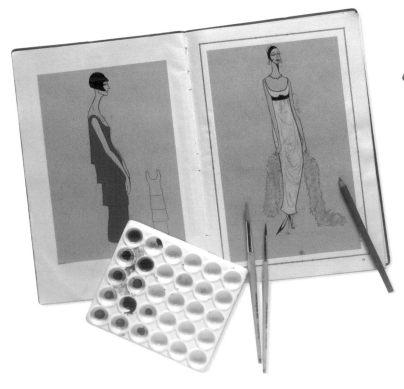

The naturalistic style requires skill in drawing and a considerable knowledge of human anatomy.

The naturalistic style allows for a moderate degree of stylization, but there is always a close connection to academic drawing.

PSYCHOLOGICAL STYLE

In what is called the psychological style the stylization of the figure reaches its ultimate expression, far removed from realist canons, and favouring simplification, abstraction and even, in some cases, caricature. These are very ingenious, creative figures.

SIMPLIFIED STYLE

The figure is reduced to a minimum in order to magnify the clothing. The head is represented with just an oval, the arms and legs are simple brushstrokes or one thin line. This illustration gets away from the silhouetted forms, volumes modelled with shading and other anatomical details.

DECORATIVE STYLE

This type of illustration pursues purely aesthetic goals. All the styling is aimed at producing a specific visual effect of great decorative value. Under this heading can be included advertising illustration, with its high level of aesthetic content, in which the originality and brilliance of the drawing take precedence over an explicit representation of the dress.

In the psychological style the artistic impulse outweighs any representation of the garment. The degree of stylization is so extreme that it is difficult to imagine the dress.

Under decorative style can be included the tendency to turn the figures into little dolls, stylized figures, usually with very large eyes and heads that remind us of toys.

An example of the simplified style, in which figures are represented with nothing but an oval and a few lines.

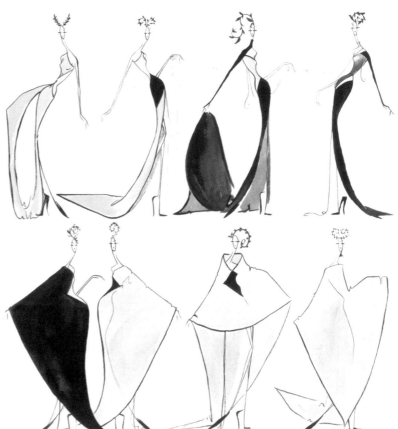

The decorative style is the one closest to the language of advertising. It is wholly subordinated to ingenious drawing with high levels of stylization.

The computer in design

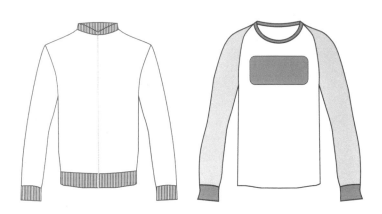

The computer is often used for flat designs, the working drawings that are sent to the sewing workshop. The drawing is clearer and the colours can be more precisely adjusted.

Hand drawings can be scanned, digitalized and coloured with the computer.

Nowadays it is not enough to have talent and know how to show it in your creations. You also need to be familiar with the digital tools available, the programs for computer-assisted design that range from specialized applications to other graphic design applications that have been adapted for the creation of clothing.

A GOOD WAY TO FINISH PROJECTS

Working with sophisticated computer systems can help evolve the style and the final treatment of colours and textures in the illustration. For today's graphic designers this is the most important medium of expression, and most of them work almost exclusively with computers. Instead of the mouse, many designers prefer a graphic palette, which makes it possible to draw and paint directly on the computer screen with a pen that is sensitive to pressure.

Working with a computer should not be a substitute for the paintbox but a useful extra tool that can help you to finish projects with great precision, particularly when working on the flat drawing and the technical specifications.

SCANNED DRAWINGS

Hand drawings with pencils or paints can be scanned into the computer and stored as picture files. On scanning a fashion figure it is converted into a digitalized image. With the help of appropriate programs you can optimize your designs, modify or colour areas that have already been painted once, and protect areas with masks or with real fabrics. The computer can be a great help if the customer asks you to modify or change some details as you will not waste so much time redoing things. Scanned line drawings can, with the aid of a printer, be turned into useful templates for working with. The number of duplicates you want can be printed out and you can make variations by turning, lengthening or distorting the image.

WORKING WITH PATTERN DESIGN

The most popular forms of illustration by computer are technical drawings and specifications. Both are necessary to the design process because they are less likely than a drawing to be misinterpreted by the manufacturer. The computer becomes a basic tool when doing working drawings, particularly the ones that will go to the sewing workshop. They are very important in the entire process of working with patterns: for filling in the pattern, the creation of the colour or vectorial pattern, creating symmetries in drawing flat garments, in the creation of the pattern on a bitmap or vectorial map, producing serialized samples of prints (particularly kaleidoscopic prints), applying a scanned texture or material to a design and in the automatic reduction of colours.

Illustration using the computer makes it possible to achieve high levels of artistic quality. Most illustrators use the graphic palette to obtain the same precision that can be achieved with traditional drawing media. Illustration by Javier Dovaler.

Using the computer you can create illustrations with interesting print effects that are difficult to obtain manually. Illustration by Marta Marqués.

VECTORIAL LANGUAGE AND BITMAPS

Once the hand drawing has been translated into a digital image the designs, figures, illustrations and patterns can be sent anywhere in the world, thanks to the Internet, with great speed and without losing quality. This makes it possible for manufacturers to adapt original designs to different sizes. There are two basic systems for processing the digital image: vectorial language and the bitmap. Vectorial language is suitable for drawings with fine, gentle lines without serrated angles or blurry images. Vectorial files take up little memory, so quality is not sacrificed for the sake of size. The images of bitmaps are made up of pixels, which is a better system for reproducing the refined details of tone and colour. The principal disadvantage of bitmaps is the large amount of memory these files take up.

Technical matters

'WHEN PEOPLE DRESS THEY DON'T THINK ABOUT THE PROCESS THAT THE CLOTHES THEY ARE WEARING GO THROUGH. THEY DON'T KNOW ABOUT THE DIFFICULTIES INVOLVED IN THE FIRST STEPS OF DESIGN, THE SELECTION OF THE FABRIC AND THE LINE AND THE POSITIONING OF THE PIECES OF THE PATTERN, THE INCREDIBLE FEELING OF CUTTING THE CLOTH, THE UNION OF ABSTRACT COMPONENTS AND THE CREATION OF THE FINAL GARMENT. FOR ME EACH STEP IN THIS PROCESS IS SPECIAL.'
Charlie Watkins, fashion designer

From the artistic to

VANESA GONZÁLEZ
PROJECT FOR A COLLECTION INSPIRED BY EGYPT, 2003
GOUACHE AND FELT-TIP PEN ON A SHEET OF PAPYRUS.

the industrial

Once a definitive project has been approved, it is now the moment to begin the industrial fashion process in the dressmaking workshops, since the final objective of any fashion design is to produce clothing. The most creative and artistic designs are delivered to the workshop along with technical specifications, which include flat drawings. This means leaving aside pictorial effects, textures and poetic or suggestive designs to produce a drawing of a cold, linear, measured, specific and detailed nature. The most fantastic ideas and the most stylish drawing techniques are of no use at all if you are not capable of representing each garment effectively. For that reason your artistic work needs to be backed up with professional specifications.

Presenting the design to a customer

The most convenient way to present your work is in a large portfolio case, which is handy and portable.

When you have spent some years working in the fashion world, you will be able to fill a portfolio with illustrations of your work that have been printed in fashion magazines, leaflets or exhibition catalogues.

For a fashion designer, showing your work to its best advantage is the most important thing of all. Go to any interview with samples that you have put in good order in a book or plastic portfolio, in order to ensure that your presentation is as professional as possible. Always keep in mind that in the fashion business first impressions count.

FORMATS FOR YOUR PRESENTATION

The best way to present your work is by using portfolio cases that are sold for this purpose. These cases have plastic covers inside to protect the work. They are available in various sizes, the most useful being A3 and A4. Remember that if you have to present a project to several customers your case needs to be big enough for all of them to see it. They are easy to carry, even when they are full, since they have a comfortable, sturdy handle on the top.

You will need to have cases of different sizes. Some will be useful to keep work in and others for presentations.

ORIGINAL AND PRINTED WORK

If you have not yet had much experience in the world of fashion you can put together a book using original illustrations, projects or collections that you have produced in design school. Just be sure that any work you present is clean in appearance and it should always seem new. By the time you have been working for a few years, these originals can be replaced by designs of yours that have been printed or published in leaflets, magazines or fashion catalogues and that give an idea of your professional background.

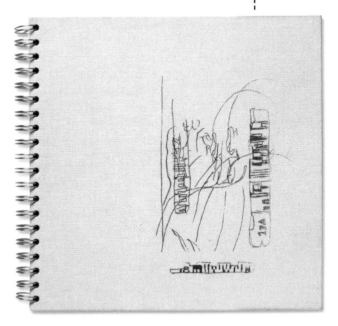

You can include samples of your designs printed on special formats to complete a portfolio of your work, like this leaflet for a fashion show.

LAYOUT OF THE VISUAL MATERIAL

A simple presentation is more likely to be a successful one since it is essential to present your ideas clearly, though a more creative style of presentation can also have a strong impact. However, avoid trying to seem excessively ingenious in the arrangement or distribution of your images. It is not advisable to overload each page, since this can prevent your ideas from flowing smoothly. If you have worked on a series of fashion figures ensure that the paper is always the same size and that the proportions of the models are consistent between each other. If the fabric in a design is complicated it is better to offer a detailed view or a sample of the material.

AVOID UNNECESSARY ADORNMENTS

The selection of images that go to make up a portfolio is made in the hope that any customers seeing your creations for the first time will be impressed by your work, the originality of the garments and the quality of the drawings. To make sure that the customer's attention is drawn to these aspects, avoid adding too many graphic effects, adornments and colour backgrounds.

Decorative elements should never distract attention from the illustrations, and colour backgrounds should not be used without a good reason, for instance when by way of contrast they bring out some aspects of the design of the clothing.

You can also prepare books in a small, easy to handle format. These formats permit you to be more creative and to prepare a more original presentation.

If you have the opportunity, include photographs of some of your designs in the portfolio.

Technical specifications

In order to avoid problems in finishing the project in the workshop, illustrations are generally accompanied by detailed, two-dimensional line drawings known as specifications, technical drawings or working drawings.

TECHNICAL SPECIFICATIONS

The final creative illustrations of the collection often need to be backed up by clear and precise working drawings that present articles of clothing in isolation, never forming a group. They are drawn as if they were laid out on the flat surface of a table. A couple of drawings are generally done of the garment, front and back views, though if the piece is complex a representation of the profile is also included. Working drawings should effectively communicate the precise production, proportion and adornment of the design, so that when it is handed over to a pattern designer or seamstress in the workshop you can be sure that your ideas will be recreated exactly.

Technical drawings for a garment do not have any degree of exaggeration or styling. They are shown as precisely as possible, in proportion and without shading to avoid misinterpretation during the process of production.

THE BEST WAY OF DRAWING

The best way of practising producing these drawings is to take garments that have already been made and stretch them out on the floor or on a coat rack, properly arranged and without creases. Then make a proportional pencil drawing which includes details of the seams, frills, position of the pockets, neckline and the shape of the sleeves. The definitive drawing is gone over with a fine felt-tip pen. The treatment is entirely linear. It does not show colours, prints or textures. It is interesting to observe how the process of producing technical drawings makes you think more deeply about the designs, since you have to make decisions about many questions that would otherwise be open to many possible interpretations.

Many technical drawings are done with computer support, which ensures the symmetry of the garment. Colour applications are also very quick and simple.

MOD. 58	DIVINAS PALABRAS HOME Crew neck sweater

SEASON. Winter 02-03   YARN   2/15 to 2 yarns Santorini (Macre, S.L.)
CHART _____   MATERIAL Smooth knit gg.5 (Mibet's)
COMP. 50% wool   FINISHED PIECE _____
      30% nylon   TAILORING   Loreto
      20% angora   PRINTING   Llach
                     EMBROIDERY _____

SIZE M

Collar 2 x 1 of 2.5 cm

Cuffs 2 x 1 of 2.5cm wide

OBSERVATIONS:

Working drawings must be very precise, clean and polished and linear. The felt-tip pen is the best medium for this kind of representation.

GETTING USED TO WORKING IN TWO DIMENSIONS

You will already be accustomed to drawing in two dimensions in your sketchbook. Working with the garments laid flat helps you to visualize them more clearly, develop ideas relating to the shape, fit, and possible combinations and layers of garments to develop a uniform and versatile collection. The garments are extended over the pages in succession, in a series, as if in a shop window. Then you can add some colour or mark the sketches you are most satisfied with and those that contain elements that are worth doing new, detailed drawings for, in order to investigate their possibilities more fully. When drawing, remember to think as much about the back view as about the front of the designs.

A DESIGN FOR THE WORKSHOP

You may work with companies in which the designer has direct contact with the workshop for pattern design, cutting, dressmaking and ironing. If you deal closely with these professionals you can communicate directly with them about the way you want the garment to be made up, in addition to the technical specifications, which bring together all the essential information. This ongoing dialogue makes it possible to carefully supervise every aspect of manufacture and prevent any detail going unnoticed. But this is not always the case. Many companies work with external workshops, and the designer has no direct contact with them apart from telephone or e-mail. Fashion drawings are seldom done, and most drawings are included in the technical specifications, which should contain as much information as possible to make the work go more smoothly.

Practise line drawing in pencil. Select a few things from your wardrobe and try to capture them in a few lines.

Using felt-tip pens of varying thicknesses can help you get across more information in the technical specifications.

Technical specifications should be shown alongside the creative designs. Elements should be drawn very clearly, offer precise proportions and determine the location and type of hems, pockets and adornments. If necessary they can be accompanied by a brief text with indications.

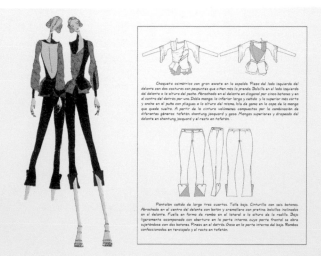

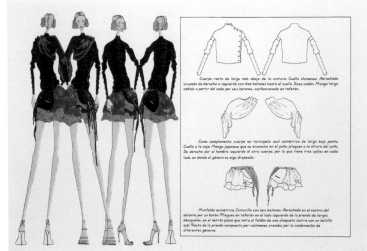

Benchmarks and scales of measurement

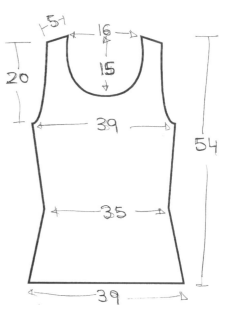

This chapter deals with the real measurements all the various parts of a garment should have. Though there is a standardized, international size table, the designer should include the definitive measurements in the technical drawing or in an additional flat drawing, since they are part of the design itself.

THE RIGHT SIZE FOR THE MARKET

Manufacturers sell garments in a range of sizes depending on the market segment they are aimed at, since fashions for young people and fashions for middle-aged people have different requirements. The diversity is even greater if you take into account that today many companies offer extra-large sizes, ranges for short and tall people or specific garments such as trousers that are sold with different leg lengths. Given the diversity of different sizes offered by the market, what is the most suitable size for a designer to work to? When a fashion student works on a project or a designer prepares an exclusive design, the most usual sizes to work with are UK sizes 10 and 12.

Certain garments require special measurements. This should be reflected in the technical specifications or in the flat drawing that is attached to the design.

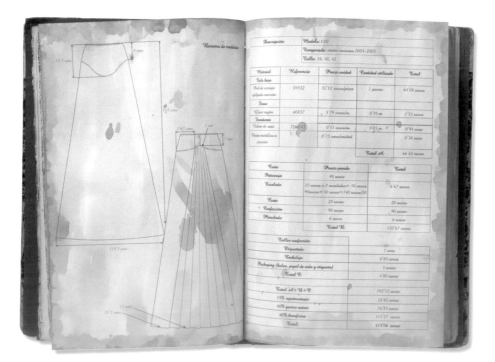

Specification drawings used for factory production are highly technical and detailed. As well as the representation of the garment, they include a detailed list with the scale of measurements.

STANDARDIZED SIZE TABLE WITH VARIATIONS

Designers do not always include a scale of measurements in their technical specifications or working drawings. In these cases the designs are projected to scale and in proportion, which acts as a guideline for the workshop. The scales of measurements used for most garments are standard, which means that they are within a specific size table. Despite this, each company, within that standardization, works to slight variations in the size table, which means that there are often slight differences in measurements in clothes of the same size made by different companies. In the same way the designer can include notations in the technical specifications on a specific measurement, for example: 'to be created using measurements established for size 14'. Other measurements that need to be estimated by the designer, such as the length of a skirt, must also be reflected in the technical specification.

MAKING A PROTOTYPE

Sometimes the designer creates his or her own pattern and even makes the prototype or original garment, so that detailed technical specifications are not necessary, since with the prototype any workshop has all the necessary information to make other identical garments. For making prototypes, various methods have been developed to measure the body for tailoring. Templates or blocks based on the division of the body into symmetrical sections are used.

It is advisable to have some basic knowledge of pattern design in order to make up most garments. Though you are probably not intending to become an expert pattern cutter, you do need to understand the importance of measurement and how to transfer these measurements to a pattern in order to create your drawings. However, it is always more effective to present the prototype to the workshop together with complete technical specifications that provide the different measurements used on it.

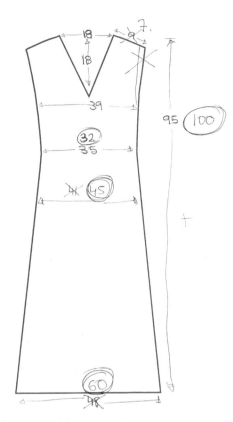

Many garments conform to standardized measurements. With skirts, dresses and trousers, however, the designer has more freedom to play with lengths.

Technical specifications of a sweater. The size (M) is specified and some observations are added as to the measurements of the neck and the seams of the sleeves and cuffs.

Instead of preparing technical specifications a prototype can be made to be delivered to the dressmaking workshop along with detailed drawings and fabric samples.

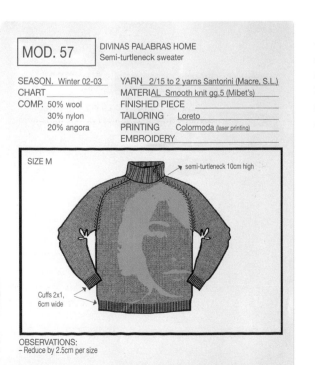

MOD. 57	DIVINAS PALABRAS HOME
	Semi-turtleneck sweater

SEASON. Winter 02-03
CHART _____
COMP. 50% wool
    30% nylon
    20% angora

YARN 2/15 to 2 yarns Santorini (Macre, S.L.)
MATERIAL Smooth knit gg.5 (Mibet's)
FINISHED PIECE _____
TAILORING Loreto
PRINTING Colormoda (laser printing)
EMBROIDERY _____

SIZE M

→ semi-turtleneck 10cm high

Cuffs 2x1, 6cm wide

OBSERVATIONS:
– Reduce by 2.5cm per size

Sewing symbols

Zigzag or overlock of two materials (A).

Flat seam for two materials (B).

Joining of two materials (C).

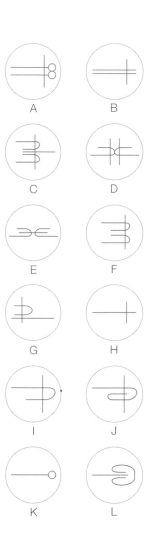

It is important that technical specifications are clear and easily understandable and contain all the information necessary for producing patterns or making the garment. For that reason, in addition to the attached texts and notes with all the necessary descriptions, sewing symbols are added.

THE FINISHES AND SEAMS OF THE GARMENT

Each sewing symbol corresponds to a type of seam and should appear along with the drawings in the technical specifications. These are specific instructions for the dressmaking workshop that define the finishes of the garment. These are universally recognized and indicate to the workshop how the finishes and seams of the garment are to be produced. It is a good idea to study these symbols in order to be able to identify each one for a particular seam, since they are basic requirements for suitable treatment of the fabric. It is also important to analyse whether the material selected is correct for the purpose assigned to it or whether a particular seam is the most suitable for a given fabric.

The international code of symbols that distinguish the seams of a garment. This is a world-recognized standard that provides the workshop with information on the finishes of the garment.

Open seam with double load (D).

Open flat seam (E).

French seam (F).

Reinforced flat seam (G).

Flat seam of one material (H).

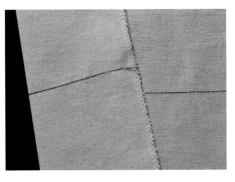

Simple hem (I).

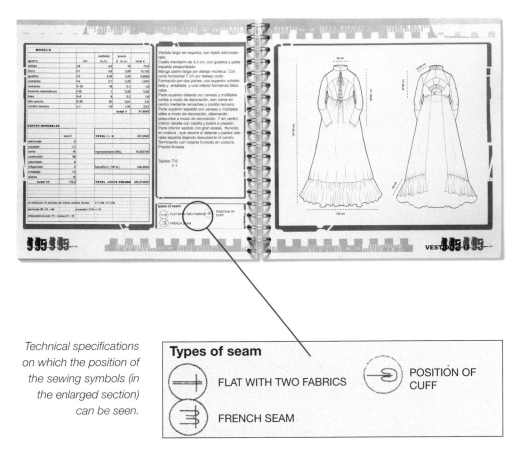

Technical specifications on which the position of the sewing symbols (in the enlarged section) can be seen.

Types of seam

FLAT WITH TWO FABRICS

POSITION OF CUFF

FRENCH SEAM

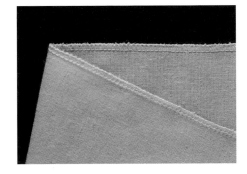

Turned hem (J).

Zigzag or overlock of a single material (K).

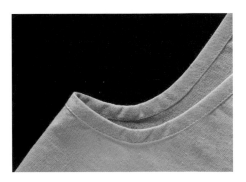

Positioning of a bias (L).

Visual fashion

ÁNGEL FERNÁNDEZ
FOUR GARMENTS FROM A COLLECTION, 2004
LINE DRAWING WITH FINE BLACK FELT-TIP PEN ON PAPER.

glossary

Throughout history fashion design has developed different silhouettes, lines, styles and finishes for each garment, though there are some common formal solutions, from which a number of variations according to the requirements of each season can be designed. In the following section examples of these different styles are set out, using clear line drawings with precise details, accentuated with clean, simple lines. Each representation is accompanied by the technical terminology by which that style is defined. This will enable you to study each of the key factors that determine the styling of a garment in isolation, which helps you to identify and distinguish them more efficiently.

Collars and necklines

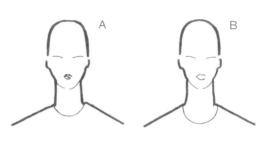

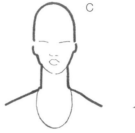
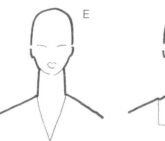
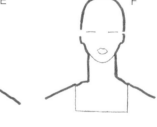

These drawings are based on a few lines made with a couple of black, fine point felt-tip pens to clearly define the forms, types and finishes of different collars and necklines. Each form of neckline or collar is determined by the fabric used, the season or occasion, and how the garment is fastened. These descriptive drawings are very useful for the stylist or designer who can learn to associate each type with the name that defines it.

Necklines
A. Box neckline
B. Round
C. Oval
D. Boat neck
E. V-neck
F. Square
G and H. Trapezoid

Knitted collars
A. High or turtleneck
B. Loose cowl
C. Turtleneck buttoned to one side

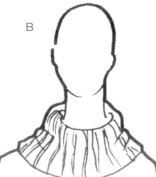
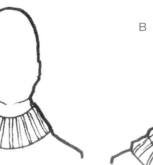

Collars

A. Shirt collar with neckband
B and C. Different collar openings
D. Collar with placket
E and F. Neckband collar
G. Peter Pan collar
H. Mandarin collar
I. Tuxedo or shawl collar
J. Shirt collar with lapel
K. Tailored collar with lapel

A
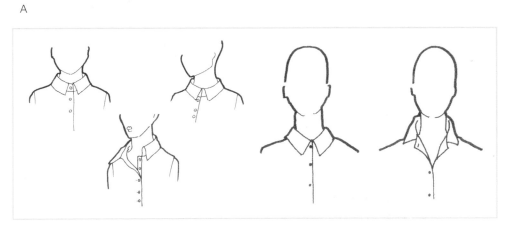

B
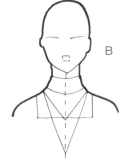

C

D
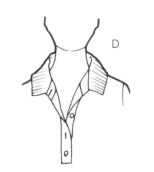

E
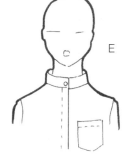

F
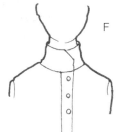

G
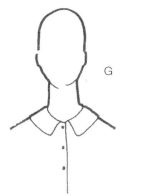

H
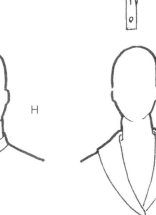

I

J

K
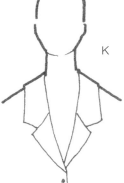

Necklines for dresses

A. Turned boat neck
B. Loose collar
C. Tailored collar with lapel
D. Turtleneck

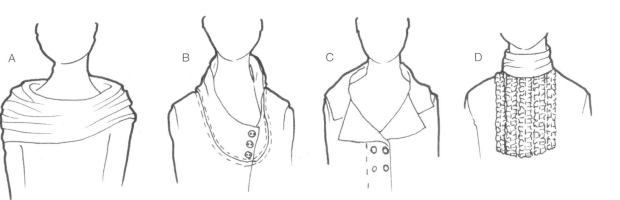

Shoulders and sleeves

The shape of the top of the sleeve, where it is joined at the shoulder to the body of the garment, and the finishing of the cuffs, are important for modifying the silhouette. As with collars there are very common types of shoulders and sleeves and it is a good idea to analyse them in isolation using line drawings. The folds or textures are either left out or simplified, reducing them to a minimum, in order to better explain the shape, line and finish of the garment.

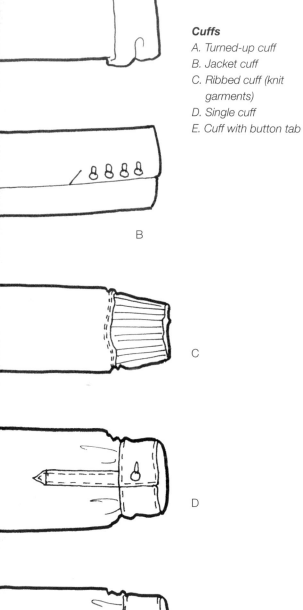

Cuffs
A. Turned-up cuff
B. Jacket cuff
C. Ribbed cuff (knit garments)
D. Single cuff
E. Cuff with button tab

Shoulders
A. American shoulder
B. Shoulder with circular flounce
C. Shoulder with drape
D. Gathered puffed shoulder

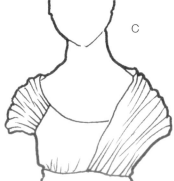

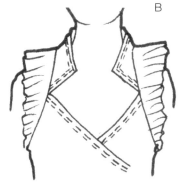

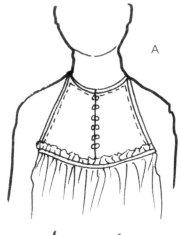

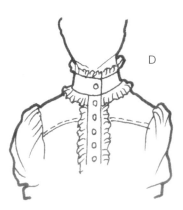

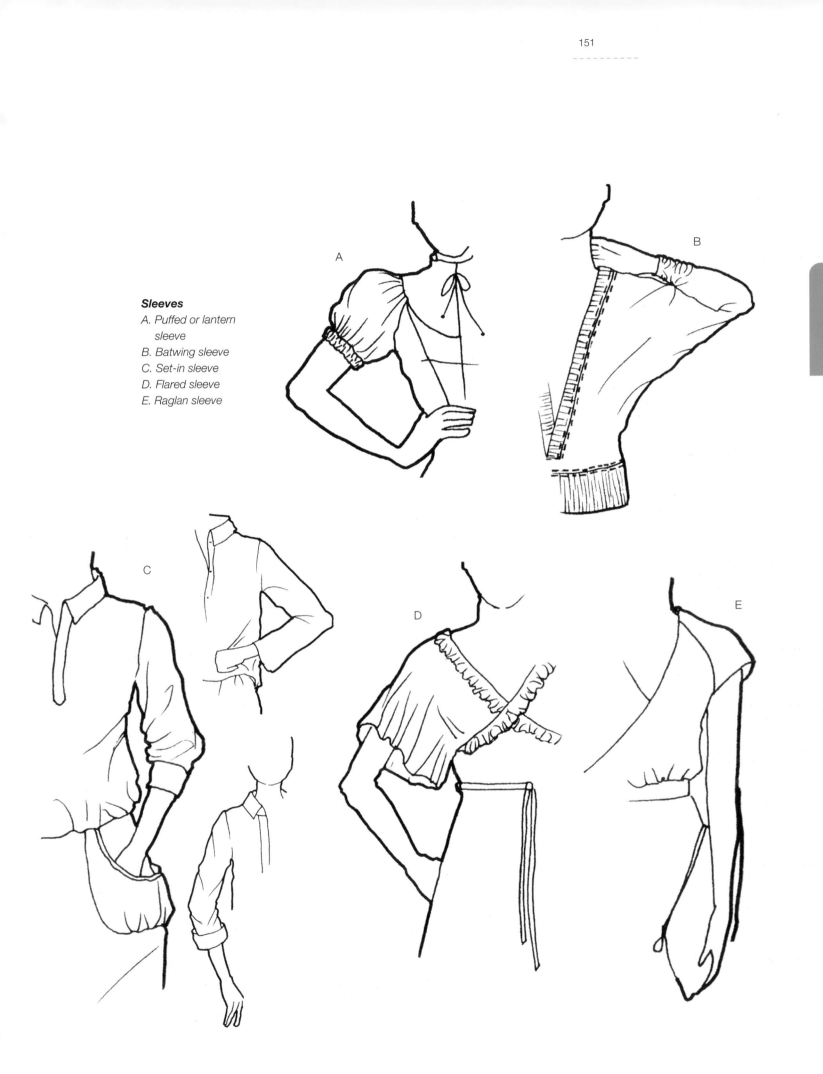

Sleeves
A. Puffed or lantern
   sleeve
B. Batwing sleeve
C. Set-in sleeve
D. Flared sleeve
E. Raglan sleeve

Blouses, dresses, shapes and finishes

On this double page different garments are represented in clear, flat drawings according to their shape and form of fastening, along with different options for finishes and adornments. Technically, finishes are all the details that characterize the model (folds, flounces, gathers, drapes, collars, pockets, etc.). The details make the garment unique and fully developed.

Practising these line drawings is a basic requirement for students who are starting out as stylists.

A. Blouse with high neck
B. Top with oval neckline and dropped armhole
C. Blouse with heavy flounce collar
D. Top with shoulder straps and sash
E. Double-breasted blouse
F. Sweater with batwing sleeves
G. Long jacket with yoke shoulders
H. Patchwork bolero with hood
I. Jacket with multiple intaglio cuts
J. T-shirt with raglan sleeves
K. Short-sleeved blouse with Peter Pan collar
J. T-shirt with kangaroo pocket and drawstring waist
M. Dress with split tiered skirt
N. Dress with gathered flounces

A

B

C

Trousers and skirts

A

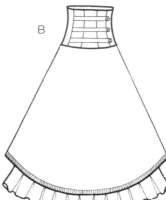

B

The following visual glossary covers trousers and skirts. Each drawing shows the silhouette, the finish, the direction and quality of the folds, the final stitches, the zips or buttons and any other detail necessary for a correct interpretation of the model. The body, the length of the skirts or trousers, the width of the sleeves and position of the pockets must be correctly proportioned. In these drawings the spacing and real amount of buttons corresponds, though in smaller size, to a real scale.

C

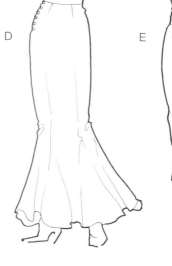

D

E

Skirts

A. Puffed skirt with gathers

B. Double-layered skirt with high
   waist

C. Full skirt

D. Skirt with godets

E. Straight or calf-length skirt

F. Full skirt

G. Skirt with sunray pleats

H. Draped tulip skirt

I. Culottes

F

G

H

I

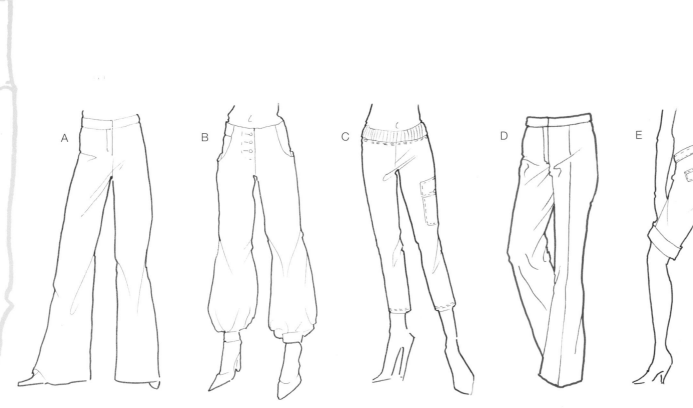

Trousers

A. Wide trousers

B. Baggy trousers

C. Cigarette pants

D. Flared trousers

E. Flap pockets

F. Shorts

G. Track pants

H. Capri pants

I. High-waisted shorts with
   straps

J. High-waisted pants with
   straps and placket and
   pockets

K. Bermuda shorts

L. Patchwork trousers

M. Indian or pyjama trousers

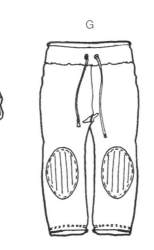

Step by step

'IN THE FACTORY THERE ARE ALWAYS PILES OF MATERIALS, COLOURS, SILHOUETTES AND SHAPES, AND WE EXPERIMENT. IDEAS? YOU GET THEM CONSTANTLY. A SOURCE OF INSPIRATION IS ART AND LIFE ITSELF.'
CUSTO DALMAU

1

2

Drawing a fashion figure

The first step to a successful drawing of an undressed female figure is to block in the figure. If the initial scheme is correctly established, with well-defined and properly proportioned shapes, finishing the outline of the figure and adding body and facial features is easy. If the blocking is not properly done in the first place, it is difficult to rectify the figure while it is being drawn.

1. The blocking in of the figure begins with the head, drawing with an HB pencil. An oval marks the starting point. Drawing a cross on it will help to position the level of the eyes. With a slanted straight line, mark the level of the shoulders and then with simple lines, go on to mark the outline of the torso and the position of the breasts.

2. A new curve describes the slight twist of the body. With another diagonal line, show the angle of the hip, which usually turns in the opposite direction to that of the shoulders. Go down the body to the legs, which are portrayed with a simple outline. The feet are shown as on tiptoe, as if wearing high heels.

3. Once the entire figure has been drawn in a schematic, sketchy fashion, fix the outline by using a 2B graphite pencil to draw new lines over the previous ones. Just as before, the process begins with the head, goes down the body and defines it as you proceed. Facial features are simple and rather stylized but effective.

3

4. The pressure on the pencil is greater than during the blocking-in phase. The objective is to make the outer profile of the figure more exact and specific, giving special attention to the sinuous feminine curves. The lines should be firm and done with a single stroke to avoid shortened or overlapping lines or hesitant strokes that might spoil the drawing.

5. The drawing of the figure is finished. This is a line drawing, without any shading. The structural lines of the blocking in phase are still visible and have to be erased. In this case the best thing to do is to use an eraser stick in order to work with more precision. Now the figure can be photocopied or traced onto other pieces of paper. After that, different dresses can be drawn or painted on top of it.

To brush away bits of eraser do not run your hand over the drawing in case you smudge the paper. Use a soft brush instead.

4

5

Drawing a figure in ink

If you are going to draw a fashion figure solely with lines of Indian ink you need to learn how to use the brush and to control the pressure in order to draw the outlines with delicacy. The most suitable line is modulated, presenting variations in the thickness of the stroke depending on whether you are drawing a lit area, a delicate one, a rounded fold or a profile in shadow. For this exercise all that is required is a graphite pencil, a bottle of Indian ink and a fine, round brush.

1. The first objective is to capture the pose in proportion. Make an effort to represent the posture of the body with a simple sketch: an oval for the head, a long, narrow and stylized neck, the curve of the back and triangular position of the arm. These first lines should perform an exclusively structural function, not a descriptive one. The entire operation is done with an HB graphite pencil.

2. On a simplified scheme of the body it is easier to draw the definitive shapes of the model. As in previous cases, draw from top to bottom, starting with the head, which is given highly stylized features, and going down over the shoulders to reach the hips. With another line outline the breasts and the curve of the belly. The figure appears thinner and more elongated than in real life.

3. When the drawing of the figure is finished the degree of stylization is evident. The neck and arms are much longer than normal, the waist is extremely narrow and the profile presents lines that are exaggeratedly curved. All these options are valid if they improve the aesthetic appearance of the figure without prejudicing the representation of the dress.

1

2

3

4. It is now time to begin the representation of the dress. It is fitted to the silhouette, coinciding with the contours of the figure. Emphasize this by pressing harder on the pencil. Pay attention to details, to the lace on the straps, filled in with a tightly curved scribble, and to the pattern, which is lightly sketched as a series of circles closely grouped together.

5. Go over the pencil drawing with a fine, round, soft-bristled brush and undiluted Indian ink. Pressure should be minimal; the bristles of the brush should hardly bend at all in order to obtain very fine strokes, particularly in the facial features. With the hair the brushstrokes are slightly thicker, in order to highlight the quiff.

6. The lines that describe details inside the figure should be soft and finer than those that make up the outer profile. The contours of the figure are emphasized with thicker and more sharply defined brushstrokes. The flounces of the dress are finished with a zigzag of rounded shapes. This stroke is done only once, just scarcely bending the tip of the brush. The lines that shape each side of the arm are also made with a single movement, a single stroke for the entire arm.

4

5

6

It is important to learn to control the pressure applied with the tip of the brush. You can practise on a separate piece of paper. It is a matter of producing fine lines that are capable of expressing delicacy or texture and other, stronger ones to reinforce the profile of the figure.

7. Draw the outline of the bent arm just as you drew the extended arm. The hands are merely suggested; it is not necessary to draw them in detail since they do not provide any information that is important to the design.

The same thing occurs with the jacket hanging from one hand. It is represented with just a few lines that provide no information as to its form or texture.

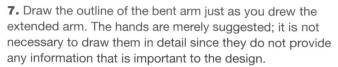

8. All the attention is now focused on the dress, on its details, finishes and texture. The pencil spots are filled in with thick black ink.

9. Let the ink dry before going on, in order to avoid smearing the colour by brushing it with the hand.

10

It is not easy to control brush work, particularly if it needs to be clean, exact and of variable thickness. It is advisable to practise drawing different aspects of the figure on separate pieces of paper, as a test, before tackling the definitive drawing.

10. The preliminary scheme gives way to a figure with clear, perfectly defined outlines. The treatment is totally linear; there is no wash or halftones to give shading effects. It is not usual to create figures only with ink; they tend to be combined with colouring effects. However, this step-by-step analysis is important in order to be able to analyse, without the interference of dealing with colour, the treatment of the outlines of the figure with a modulated line. If you cannot successfully handle monochrome figures like this one, it will be difficult for you to be able to confront more complicated challenges in which more colours are involved.

Using hatching

Purely linear drawings are the most difficult for the designer, since texture and shadow need to be dealt with without using colouring or wash. This exercise shows you how to design a dress combining different types of hatching. It is a good idea to practise this, since each type of hatching conveys a specific sort of information on the the drawing. To carry out this step-by-step process all you need are three coloured pencils: black, brown and red.

1

2

3

1. Up to now the fashion figures in this book have been fairly naturalistic, with only a small degree of stylization. Now the figure is going to be given a considerable amount of distortion. To draw it in a balanced way first draw a straight vertical line that divides the paper in two. In this way you will prevent the pose leaning to one side and looking unbalanced.

2. Draw your first lines with the brown pencil, starting with the head. This time the oval is quite small in relation to the body. The back and arm are bent in a quite exaggerated fashion. The body is short, leaning backwards and the legs, though unfinished at this stage, look as if they are going to be extremely long.

3. Once you have established the degree of stylization in the figure, go over the contours of the figure with a different pencil, then draw in the hat and the features of the face. The legs seem extremely bent, the waist is extraordinarily slim and the thighbone very short.

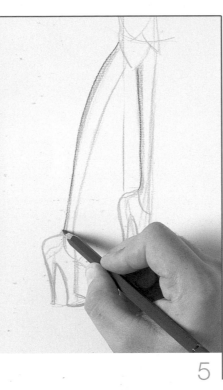

4 | 5

If you work with figures in profile it is a good idea to twist the body a little to avoid it becoming too rigid and lacking in dynamism.

4. With a very sharp black pencil complete the headdress of feathers on top of the hat using a hatching of curved lines. Put more pressure on the upper part and a bit less on the lower. With a scribble indicate the texture of the hat. Using gentle lines, with hardly any pressure, finish the eyes and establish the location of the nose, indicated with just two dots.

5. When you are drawing a dress that will have prominent hatching with black lines, the outline of the figure needs to be emphasized more than usual. Supposing that the light on the model comes from the right, accentuate the left profile with the red pencil. In this way you obtain a contrast in tone between the two profiles that acts as a basic indication of shading.

6. The concept of working on the outline of the figure with two analogous colours of differing intensity is extended over the rest of the body. The model's face becomes an important focus of attention. It is the only part of the body that is profiled in red on both sides. The few indications of the dress still seem sketchy. This is because it is not a good idea to work on the dress without first having resolved the problems of the figure.

6

7. Having completed the figure it is time to tackle the dress. First draw the shape, the cut and the components with the black pencil. On the skirt the folds formed in the lower part are more intense. The same occurs with the strokes that define the neckline and the waist. With the same scribble used on the hat, darken the glove. The shoes are only outlined.

8. The real work begins here. Recreate the pattern and the texture of the dress by working solely with hatching with black lines. Before doing any hatching, decide in which direction the lines should be going in each section. Thus the bodice is made up with evenly spaced crossed lines. On the skirt the cross-hatching is more uniform and slightly closer together on the left, since this is the side in shadow.

9. The skirt is distinguished from the bodice by a tone that is generally darker. This is obtained by pressing down a bit more when drawing in the lines of the cross-hatching and applying more pressure with pencil. Then go down the figure to colour the shoes. Since the shoes are of patent leather, cross-hatching is not appropriate and so they are covered with deep black shading. Over the heel and at the tips, put in a white area to simulate the shine of the patent-leather surface.

10. On the right side of each fold, the cross-hatching gets clearer or even disappears altogether, leaving an area that indicates where the light comes from. Then go over each fold with a new, deeper line.

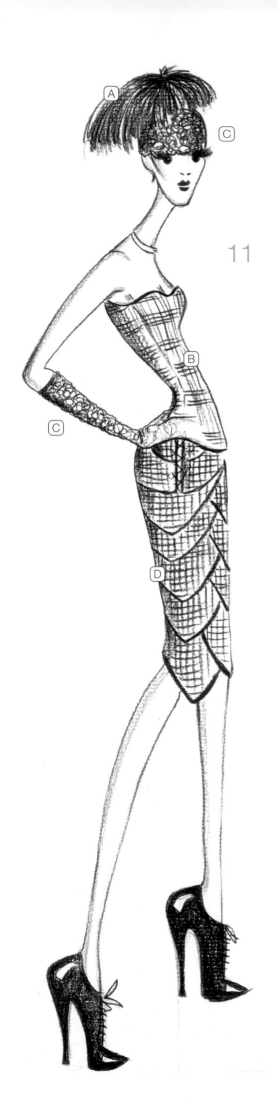

A

B

C

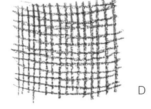

D

A gentle stroke using a graphite pencil or partially worn felt-tip pen can provide an interesting effect of soft cross-hatching on any dress. Whatever the medium, in cases where hatching is used, the outline of the dress should always be kept clearly and sharply defined.

11. With the painting of the shoes the figure appears to be complete. Now take a moment to analyse the use of the hatching on the different surfaces. The plumage of the hat has been achieved with juxtaposed curving cross-hatching without too much order (A). On the bodice cross-hatched squares have been made up of a succession of three crossed lines with a blank space between them (B). The hat and the glove have been covered with a scribble made up of small circular shapes that are suitable for representing embroidery or sequins (C). Finally, on the skirt, the hatching shows a uniform distance between the lines, with the horizontal lines shown as slightly curved to better describe the volume of the garment (D).

Using ink washes

A good way to colour quickly and effectively is to paint with wash over a template or the sketch of a figure in a fairly fluid fashion. The results look very spontaneous. In a dress with transparent areas, coloured ink washes represent the most suitable medium for colouring.

1. The structure of the figure is based on a simplified analysis of the different anatomical components. Though the figure has been stylized (the head looks small, the waistline has been reduced and the extremities lengthened), the corresponding proportions are consistent. Before starting to paint, the figure is traced on tracing paper or A4 paper that will be used as a template for new exercises.

2. Blue ink is diluted with a lot of water and, without doing a prior drawing, the paper is coloured. The tip of the brush is used to suggest the shape of the dress on the body. Moving downwards, the left profile of the body is painted in until the skirt is reached. The brush is wetted with a greater amount of wash ink and is spread, in an irregular fashion, over the skirt.

3. The wash on the skirt is shown as more intense on the left side and gets lighter, by diluting the colour more with water as it moves to the right. The brushstrokes should be long and point in the direction of the folds of the skirt. While the wash is still wet a few strokes of magenta wash are superimposed and mixed in, forming faint nuances, and the flower is painted at the neckline.

If you do not feel secure about painting the dress without a preliminary drawing, take the pencil used for the preliminary scheme and portray in detail the features and forms of the dress as in previous exercises.

4. With the wash of the skirt still a bit moist, the waistline is underscored and the left profile of the dress is painted in with a fine brush and black ink. Due to the moisture of the paper the ink spreads and blends with the underlying colours. With the same brush the facial features are constructed using brushstrokes of variable thicknesses.

5. Drawing lightly with the very tip of the brush, almost caressing the paper, the outline of the arms, the hem of the skirt and the figure's feet are finished. The lines should be fine, so take care not to load the brush with too much ink. The silhouette of the figure is marked in a dramatic way by first

moistening the left side with a brush that has nothing but water on it. Then a line is drawn on top of the moistened area with black ink. This line spreads subtly over the moist area, offering a highly contrasted gradation. When the ink dries, erase the pencil lines.

6. It is not always necessary to do a pencil drawing before colouring a figure. Here the dress and the features of the face have been painted directly with the brush. The irregularities and subtle tonal changes provided by the wash of paint are very suitable for representing clothing in which the lightness of the fabric and its areas of transparency play important roles.

4

5

6

Using coloured pencils

1

With the same fashion figure as before, which you can use as a kind of template, the next exercise shows how to create another design, which will be coloured in with coloured pencils. This is a medium that usually complements ink washes, watercolours or gouache, or work with felt-tip pens, but that here is presented in isolation in order to practise the correct way of colouring. Coloured pencils provide a soft, subtle chromatism, with gentle transitions between the colours. They are particularly suitable for delicate, light-coloured clothing.

1. Taking the sketch of the figure from the previous exercise, make a copy on another piece of paper. You can do this by making a tracing, either using tracing paper or against the light on window glass. Then, with a mechanical pencil go over the traced image again to make it sharper.

2. On the figure, draw the hairstyle and the shape of the dress, letting it adapt itself to the body as if it were a transparent veil that allows you, throughout the process, to check on its fit and harmony with the female figure wearing it. The drawing is completely linear. It is not necessary to do shading or to press too hard with the pencil.

3. With a pink pencil, go over the outline of the face, the upper part of the body and the legs. Lightly colour the left side with a clear suggestion of shading. At the moment concentrate on the flesh tones, and pay no attention to the blouse the figure is wearing. With another yellow pencil colour the hair, and use a rich brown to mark the silhouette of the skirt.

2

3

4. Superimpose the blouse on the bust of the figure. First outline its contours with the brown pencil and then colour it in with a lighter-coloured pencil. Apply the colour very gently, without pressing down on the pencil, so that it forms a transparent layer that does not completely cover the flesh tones. The colour of the hair is intensified with orangey tones and brown strokes. The lit areas are left in white.

5. Once you have finished the colouring of the upper half of the body it is time to tackle the pattern on the skirt. It is not a matter of reproducing the shapes exactly, it is sufficient to suggest them. For that purpose you can sketch in a series of juxtaposed, disorderly spirals, one on top of the other using a brown, medium tone pencil.

6. Finish the skirt by applying a dark brown shading effect to the folds on the left. In this way the skirt acquires a greater sense of volume. The last addition is the detail on the blouse. This is done with a few small, scribbled shapes.

You can experiment on the same model with different drawing media and colours to see to what extent they affect the design of the figure. Take a look at the differences between the treatment of the blouse and the pattern on the skirt with watercolor and with ink and gouache.

4

5

6

1

2

Using a patterned fabric is one of the most popular methods for making clothing more decorative. The designer needs to learn to individualize and personalize his or her own patterns. There are different techniques for representing them on the figure, but this step–by-step exercise describes the use of felt-tip pens to represent a checked jacket. The pens should be alcohol-based so you can work with glazes without the colours running accidentally when one stroke goes over another. Professional pens are best since they have a choice of heads, one with a bevelled tip and the other with a rounded, fine tip.

Using felt-tip pens

1. Make a preliminary drawing with a graphite pencil. The body of the figure is outsized, to give more space in which to create the pattern of the jacket. With a black permanent felt-tip pen go over the drawing, making broad, heavy lines where there is a fold or a lapel in relief. The work with the felt-tip pen is done with modulated lines of varying thickness, depending on whether the area is lit or shaded. On the left side of the face add in thick, regular blocked shading in black. The general appearance of the figure is reminiscent of the visual language of a comic.

2. With the drawing finished, colour in the hair and shirt with uniform tones. With a permanent marker pen, use the bevelled tip to draw horizontal stripes on the jacket. They should not be absolutely horizontal but should be slightly inclined depending on the volume of each part of the garment. The lines should be firm and done with a single stroke to avoid stops and overlapping colours. With other markers in pink and salmon add in the tie, alternating diagonal strokes with the two colours.

3. Now cover the blank spaces that were left between the previous strokes with another colour, in this case khaki green. First fill in the spaces with horizontal lines and then draw vertical lines forming a characteristic check. As in the previous case, the perpendicular lines are not straight. They curve to adapt themselves better to the shape of the jacket. The pattern should adapt itself to the volume of the body.

4. Use the fine tip of the marker pen to draw a new check (in the same pink that you used for the tie) inside the grey and khaki coloured lines. This completes the pattern of the jacket.

Before drawing the figure it is advisable to decide on the design and the colours that you are going to use in the pattern. Draw a box and then incorporate the colours little by little inside the box, until the definitive design is determined. Here you can see the sequence of development of the checked pattern used in this exercise.

5. With a grey fine-point felt-tip pen draw parallel vertical lines on the shirt. Now it is time to add some graphic touches. With the bevelled tip of the grey marker outline the right side of the figure. With a brown marker, go over the jacket lapels and some of the folds to give a hint of shading. In short, give a certain feeling of volume to a jacket that might otherwise seem too flat.

Transferring an image: fashion figure in acrylic

Acrylic painting has won itself a place in the world of fashion thanks to its vivid colours, rich textures and original pictorial effects. It is quick drying and the possibility of going over patches of colour with new opaque tones means you can rectify mistakes and try out different colourings as you work. This is convenient and diminishes the possibility of errors. In this step-by-step exercise the template of the figure used in the two previous exercises will again be used, this time to illustrate a common tracing procedure.

1

2

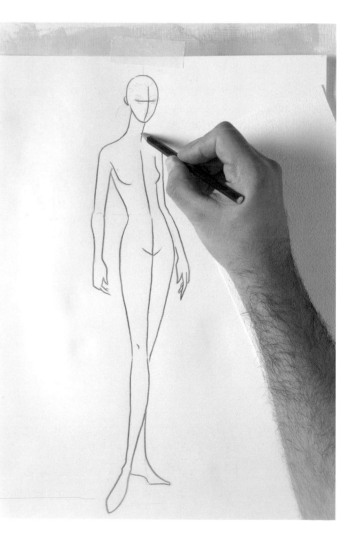

3

1. Because you are going to paint the figure with acrylic, a generally opaque medium, first prepare the background with a wash of magenta, thoroughly thinned with water. While it dries prepare the drawing of the figure to be traced.

2. The template of the figure you have saved will be traced on a coloured background. For that purpose turn over the piece of paper and redraw the lines of the inverted figure with a thick magenta pastel. It is easier if you do this on a light box or against a windowpane.

3. The piece of paper with the template is placed on top of the background colour, which is now dry. With the same graphite pencil that was used to draw the original figure, go over the lines, this time pressing down hard so that the coat of pastel sticks to the paper underneath. It is important to work with a clearly conceived drawing.

4

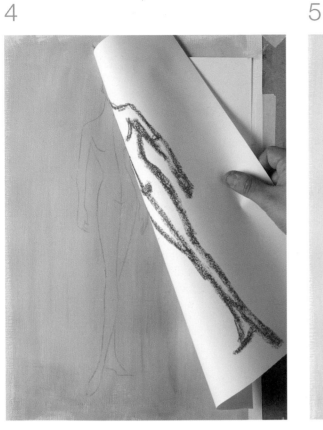

5

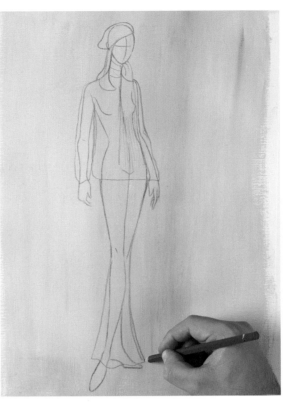

Though you are working on coloured paper with acrylics here, you do not have to use opaque paint. You can also use transparent washes and let the colour you apply blend with the background colour.

4. After going over the lines of the drawing lift the paper to check that the image has been transferred onto the paper below. The lines will be faint, but visible enough to begin to work on.

5. Starting from the transferred image build up the definitive drawing of the figure. With a thick red pencil go over the pastel lines and then add new ones to represent the clothing, which adapts itself to the body as if it were transparent.

6

6. With a round, medium brush, begin the colouring process with thick, opaque acrylic paint. Work up the flesh tones and each garment with a uniform coat of colour, without modelling or shading effects. These coats will provide the base on which the details, textures and patterns are worked.

7

7. Each garment has been represented by an apparently flat area of colour. A little brown has been added to the bottom part of the skirt to give a hint of shading, along with a touch of ochre on the right arm. The amount of paint used is quite minimal and barely perceptible.

8. Using a round, fine, soft-bristled brush, lightly blend beige with ochre and use it to darken some parts of the sweater. With a couple of strokes of burnt sienna indicate the fall of the scarf. On top of them add brushstrokes of beige to break up the line. Using ochre, apply a regular series of dots on the skirt to indicate the pattern.

8

9

9. With a fine brush steeped in brown, introduce linear elements that give more definition to the shape, outline and some details of the outfit. Add facial features and shape the hands. With the same colour, outline the feet and introduce a shadow on one side of the hat.

10

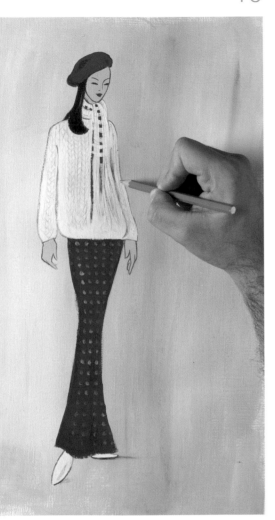

10. All that is left is to solve the problem of the texture of the knitted sweater. This is done with an ochre pencil, using a hatching of plaited lines that indicate the design of the garment. It is not necessary to draw the entire pattern so that it covers the sweater completely. It will be enough to use this textured effect in some areas.

It is best to work with a limited palette of colours. Do not attempt to use an extensive range of colours if the design does not call for it. Try to obtain your variations with just a few mixtures.

11

11. A figure that is created using gouache or acrylic has more body, so these media are best to use when the garments you are drawing are made of thick, heavy materials. You can add an aesthetic touch by painting a gentle white line along the outline of the left side of the body and projecting a soft shadow beside the foot. These graphic effects, though subtle, help to bring out the profile of the figure.

Using pastel and gouache

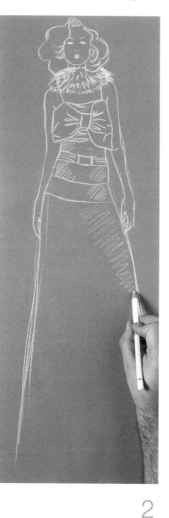

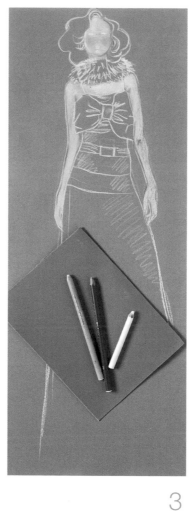

When working with pastel on Canson coloured paper you can give clothing deep, saturated colour effects. Combining the use of pastel sticks and pencils you will be able to work comfortably with lines and blocks of colour, though it is normal to mix the colours with subtle blending of tones. This medium turns out to be most suitable for dresses in a range of vivid colours, a satiny shine or a marked shading effect. Pastel is often used in conjunction with other pictorial techniques such as watercolours, acrylics or gouache.

1   2   3

1. The colour chosen for the paper is magenta, since this will harmonize best with the colouring of the dress. The drawing is done with a white pastel pencil. The process of constructing the figure has already been covered in the preceding pages, so this section will be devoted to describing the colouring phase.

2. After an initial line drawing that focuses attention on the contours of the figure, the portrayal of the limbs and the facial characteristics, you can then add in the highlights of the hair, the feathers of the collar and the first hints of light, whitening parts of the dress using the white pencil.

3. Combining three colours of pastel pencil (sienna, pink and white) paint the flesh tones of the figure with strokes that you can then merge together by rubbing with the fingertips. The white will permeate the pink in the lighter areas and the sienna will do the same in the shading. Pastel pencils make it possible to work in more detail than can be done with pastel sticks, though the latter offer better tonal quality because they have much more pure pigment in their composition.

When working with pastels, it is a good idea to avoid using stumps. It is preferable to work with the fingers. This enables you to control the blending of colours better and to always keep the drawing clean, since your hands are easier to wash than the paper.

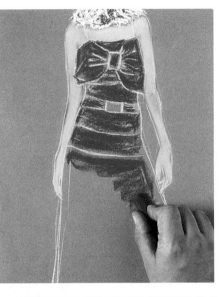

4. Paint the hair with the yellow pastel stick. Over it apply a few shadows of burnt sienna and blend it in with your fingertip. The feathers at the neck are represented with just a few untidy, superimposed strokes of white. Colour in the dress with the magenta stick, being careful not to cover the white lines that serve as guidelines for the drawing.

5. On top of the coats of magenta superimpose new patches of intense white. To thoroughly cover the area, rub with the side of the stick. To obtain the satin sheen of the material, blend the white with the underlying colour to form very delicate colour transitions. Blend it in by rubbing the painted surface with the fingertips.

6. If you analyse your dress after the colours have been blended you will see that the effect of the light you have achieved is similar to that of a photographic model. When you are happy with the drawing, make a new mixture for the feathers at the neck; this time, since working space is limited, using your little finger.

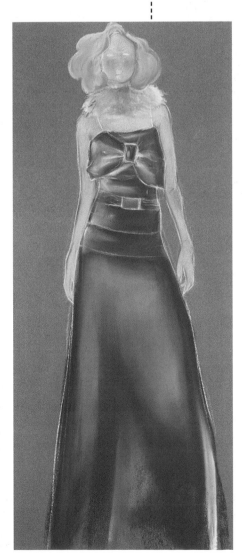

7

7. Put aside your stick and take up a black pastel pencil. The point of the pencil is ideal for the tiny details of the face, such as the shape of the eyes and eyebrows, and the contours of the face itself. The line should be thin and very subtle. It is obtained without applying pressure, almost caressing the surface of the paper with the point.

8. Having finished the work with dry pastels, use gouache to create highlights. Before painting it is advisable to set the pastel with an aerosol fixative. Wait a couple of minutes for it to dry and then pick up a fine round brush soaked in undiluted white gouache. With the tip of the brush add some highlights in the hair and the dress and some points of light on the buckles. On the feathers the brushstrokes should be very fine, moving outwards. With the same fine brush you can precisely outline the shape of the dress.

9. Continue by whitening one half of the background to provide a contrast with the silhouette. To bring out the other side of the silhouette, use another graphic alternative, profiling. To do this, paint a fine, unbroken line with black gouache, defining the contours of the body and the dress.

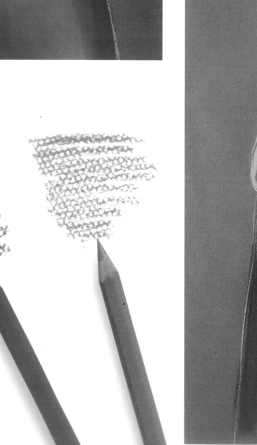

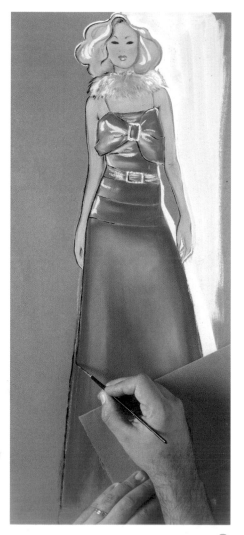

8

9

10

When working with pastel it is advisable to keep handy another piece of paper in the same colour as that of your exercise to do tests of blends, strokes, contrasts and styles of drawing. That way you can experiment with the different effects before including them in the definitive project.

Outline the figure with a fine brush, being careful not to go outside the boundaries of the shape. On the other hand, you can cover the more extensive areas of the background quickly, with a slightly thicker brush.

10. The illustration is finished. The result is very fresh and stands out due to the chromatic vitality provided by the pastel and the strong highlights in gouache. In stylizing the drawing the size of the head and the body have been reduced, making the dress longer, to emphasize the *sfumato* on the skirt, which gives a very good representation of the material, its fall, texture and sheen. This shows how important it is to know how to correctly select your drawing medium depending on the purpose of your design and the tactile quality of the material and the garment.

The theme of this project is the jellyfish, examining its organic design, its tentacles and its colours. Find some photographs that will make it possible for you to study their anatomy. You can find this information in biology books, on the Internet or in any encyclopedia. Then scan the photographs or photocopy them in colour and reproduce them in a large size in order to study them clearly.

You can draw fashion figures in different poses, in a very sketchy fashion, or you can trace them from a book on fashion drawing. Do your drawings with an HB pencil, then photocopy the figures to make templates on which to work. On the photocopied figures you can begin to prepare the initial ideas for your designs.

Project: jellyfish dress

This project forms part of a task that can take several weeks. It will be summarized here in a few pages and will cover the process of research, sketching, design and construction of a garment. It is a simulation of what a designer is expected to do when creating an article of clothing. You will see how the designer starts with a theme, studies it, analyses it, adopts its language and adapts it to the world of fashion, filtering it through his or her individual style. The goal of the project is to show the capacity of the designer to investigate a subject in a creative and suitable manner.

The sketching phase attempts to create variations on an original idea. So, using another photocopied template you can develop another idea, another dress inspired by the long, stinging arms of the jellyfish, which become the main concept of the dress, which is fitted tightly below the breasts.

Before starting work on the fashion drawing, try to draw and paint the original subject. You need to get to know its structure by means of drawing, scrutinizing each shape, each point of relief or colour effect. Fill your sketchbook with a number of drawings like these.

Again, work on another model in pencil on the photocopies. You can develop it more carefully, putting down a number of views from different angles from the front and behind. The irregular folds of the garment are reminiscent of the undulating arms that are seen on some types of jellyfish.

A. In pencil draw more figures, quite schematically and without any facial characteristics. You can photocopy them again to work on the designs in a more individualized way and note the first indications of colour. The first model presents a hood with spiral lines radiating out of it, reminiscent of the tentacles of the jellyfish. The soft tones are filled in with coloured pencils.

B. On another photocopy of the figure you can develop a new variation on the previous design. Treatment of the garment is still quite simple and the application of the colours is regular and flat. You do not need to work on details since you are still in the conception phase of the project. The range of colours used is quite limited.

C. The dress is drawn in a very sketchy way. Lines are drawn without precision, in a merely suggestive manner. What is important is the general impression of the whole, which should allow you to evaluate the suitability of the design. Colouring is also done quite rapidly. This is still in the sketching phase and will be more painstaking when it comes to the definitive illustration of the figure.

D. Here is a design that differs from the previous ones. Nonetheless, it maintains an organic line of inspiration and a choice of colours that links it to the others. It is inspired by the shape of the jellyfish's internal organs.

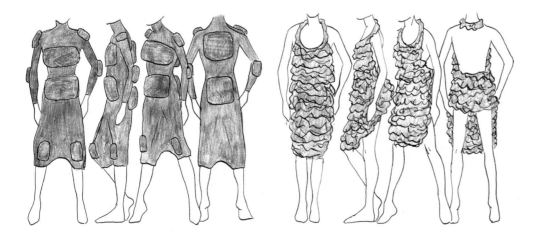

On new schematic drawings of the figures, plan different views of one or more of the models. This allows you to check the body from 360 degrees, to see how the panels of orange alter the silhouette of the figure. To check this it is not necessary to draw the head of the figure. The representation from different angles has the same purpose, to precisely describe the variation in the length of the dress. This is best understood by employing a front view, a profile, a three-quarter view and another from behind. This gives you an idea of the effect of the rotation of the body.

1

2

3

1. Once the conceptual phase has been completed, go on to draw a definitive illustration of one of the designs in this collection. Make your sketch with an HB pencil, and since in this case you are not dealing with a long dress, the framing cuts off the figure above the knees. The schematic drawing should be simple and very similar to that done in previous exercises. It is not necessary to have a model in front of you; you can draw from memory or perhaps using a photograph from a magazine as a point of reference.

2. Begin to draw the face, indicating the features and the hairstyle. You do not need to copy any specific photo, but instead work with an idealized image of a model. Dress the figure with your definitive design inspired by the jellyfish. In this case the collar is voluminous and is reminiscent of the jellyfish's head, the dress taking the form of its body and the skirt its tentacles. The dress is conceived as if it were transparent, to fit it properly over the figure.

3. Using a pencil, draw in further details of the face. Treatment is very naturalistic, without any stylization whatsoever. Intensify the outlines, since it will be necessary to see them during the colouring phase. The lower part of the dress, the skirt, is left unfinished, since it is to be finished with gestural brushstrokes, and traces of pencil lines could spoil the effect.

4

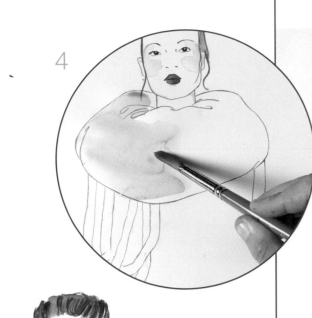

5

Before painting the illustration it is a good idea to do different colour tests on paper. The colours should be mixed together forming gradations so you can see how they combine and then choose which ones you would like to use in the project.

6

4. With a wash of brown acrylic paint and a fine, round brush, paint the hair. Use intense carmine red for the lips. With acrylic paint thinned with water to a consistency similar to that of watercolour, the garment's bulky collar is painted in, this time using a medium round brush. It is enough to apply a bit of colour and spread it by just adding water to the paper. This same wash colour is used to give a blush to the cheeks.

5. While the wash on the collar is still moist, paint an intense red and yellow on top of it. The brush should be thoroughly steeped in these colours. On touching the wet paper the colours spread out over the surface blending into one another, creating unstable contours and *sfumato*. Be careful not to go over the boundaries established by the lines done in pencil. Prepare the body of the dress in the same way. First cover it with a reddish wash that has been well thinned with water so that it soaks into and moistens the paper.

6. The operation is similar to the previous one. On the pre-painted area that is still moist, use red and yellow on the right side of the dress and add a bit of carmine and brown on the left. In this way a tonal gradation that goes from light to dark, from an orange to a red-brown, is represented, and helps give a shading effect to the illustration. The details of the bands on the left are worked on with the fine, round brush. If you want to make them more definite you only need to wait until the layer of red has dried.

7

7. Go down the paper until you reach the skirt, and stain it with a pink wash, repeating the previous procedure. Without letting the wash dry completely, make some broad, gestural strokes with a fine, round brush steeped in very slightly diluted red paint. On this wash, using the same brush, add in some diagonal cross-hatching to represent the direction in which the material of the skirt is going to go.

8. When making broad gestural strokes avoid resting the hand on the paper. The movement of the forearm must be complete in each brushstroke. This is a good way to gain control over the brushstroke when it goes a long way.

9. Check out the difference between the step-by-step exercise using acrylic from this illustration coloured with gouache. The red here is more opaque and intense and there are fewer nuances and changes of tone.

8

9

10

Some fashion drawings tend to be accompanied by more technical illustrations or drawings of details that attempt to describe a specific material or texture. This information is fundamental for avoiding confusion between the designer and the workshop.

11

10. The definitive illustration is much more informative than the initial sketches, which are only meaningful to the designer. Such sketches should not be taken into account, since they form a part of the creative process and are not meant to be informative. Here the visualization of the garment is clearer. Nonetheless, it would still be necessary to accompany the illustration with more technical drawings and fabric samples, since doubts can arise about how the skirt is to be made. The choice of material and type of padding to be used is fundamental in order for the collar to have the required shape and volume.

11. Designer Esther Rozas, 'Yosolita', made the real garment on the basis of this design. It clearly reflects the appearance of the jellyfish. In the image you can appreciate the definitive result as regards the skirt, in the form of a knit garment with pants attached underneath.

A

Acrylic fabric A synthetic fabric made from acrylic acid (propenoic). It is a tough material with a good fall and soft texture. It is used to make sweaters and sports clothes and to line boots, gloves, jackets and trainers.

B

Backstitch A stitch that is made with the stitches together, moving the needle back after each stitch to insert the thread into the same place where it has gone before.

Bias A piece of cloth cut diagonally: in other words, at a 45 degree angle to the selvage.

Brocade A heavy material made of silk woven in jacquard construction with different-coloured threads (generally forming flower or ribbon patterns) in which the warp shows raised designs.

D

Drape Material gathered at a point to control the folds formed by the fall of the fabric.

E

Embroidery Pattern made by hand or machine that is purely decorative in function. It is made with various kinds of threads.

F

Facing A fine fabric cut on the bias and used to embellish the finish of necklines, cuffs, armholes, etc.

Fall This is determined by the weight and consistency of the material as well as the way in which the dress has been manufactured. Materials made with natural fibres have a better fall than those made with artificial fabrics.

Felt A fabric made from pressing or braiding fibres such as cotton, rayon and wool. It is used for lining and to make garments stiffer and also in hats.

Flounce Piece of fabric that is gathered in a circular or spiral form on the edges of a dress to give it fullness.

Frill A narrow strip of fabric that is sewn in pleats at one of its edges, or making folds, so that it is loose on the other edge, finishing in a small ruffle. Often used to finish necklines and sleeves.

Fringe An ornamental border made up of a series of threads or cords hanging from a band of cloth.

Fullness Additional looseness or volume of a garment, which is added to the edges of the skirt, where it does not fit itself to the body, to give it more movement.

G

Gather Cloth pulled together with stitching to form puckers and parallel lines.

Groin Measurement for trousers from the waistline to the groin.

H

Hem Fold, roll or double stitch, used to finish the edges of garments.

I

Interlining Piece of fabric that is inserted between the outside fabric and the ordinary lining of a garment to reinforce it or make it firmer.

L

Lapel The front part of a blouse or jacket that is turned back on the collar.

Lycra Synthetic chemical fibre made from polyurethane elastomers. It is very elastic and strong, and is used extensively in underwear, and sportswear.

M

Modelling The action of creating drapes on a body or mannequin.

Muslin Fine, closely woven cotton fabric that is used for testing garments. When it is dyed and finished it serves as a base for a variety of types of clothing.

N

Nylon Synthetic fibre whose tensile resistance is similar to that of silk but which is more elastic.

O

Ombré Shading or colour effect that has gradual changes from light to dark, typically found in men's neckties or the materials in some women's clothing.

P

Pantone An extensive colour chart in which the colours appear with a reference number for designers and manufacturers. This colour chart is internationally recognized by the fashion industry.

Piece Each of the different parts of which a garment is made up.

Pleat Permanent fold made with an iron that can be used in most types of clothing.

Polyester Strong chemical fibre, composed of ethylene glycol and terephthalic acid. It is washable and easy to maintain, and can be mixed with other fibres to create different materials.

R

Reinforcement A piece of material that is added on the areas of most wear on the garment, or to give shape or freedom of movement to the crotch or armpit.

Rib knit A knit that is straight and close together so that there are vertical, equal ribs on both sides of the material. It is typically used for the waistlines of sweaters and also in sports socks and clothing.

Ruff An adornment, cylindrical in form, which was used as a collar, particularly during the sixteenth and seventeenth centuries.

S

Sheath dress A very tight dress which has no belt and fits the outline of the body.

Stay Metal or plastic rib with which a corset is constructed or that is set inside certain garments (to reinforce collars, bodices or seams).

T

Tatting Lace made with looped cotton or linen thread. A delicately made design used on handkerchiefs and lingerie.

Toile A very malleable, inexpensive material that is used to make up test garments before using the actual material.

Top block The distance between the crotch and the waistband.

Torso Part of the garment that goes from the shoulders to the waist.

Trunk Measurement of a garment, dress or suit that goes from the neck to the waistline, front and back.

Tuck A fold stitched or woven into the cloth for purposes of shortening, decorating or controlling fullness.

V

Vintage Term used to describe second-hand clothing, but only those that have particular class or style. In general these are antique, original and unique garments. Describes old clothes that are often combined with other, modern pieces.

W

Warp Series of vertical or lengthwise threads crossed by the weft to form a fabric.

Glossary

Bibliography

• Chuter, A. J. *Introduction to Clothing Production Management*. Blackwell Publishing, USA, 2001

• Drudi, Elisabetta and Paci, Tiziana. *Figure Drawing for Fashion Design*. The Pepin Press, Amsterdam, 2001

• Entwistle, Joanne. *The Fashioned Body: Fashion, Dress and Modern Social Theory*. Polity Press, Cambridge, 2000

• Gale, Colin. *Fashion and Textiles*. Berg Publishers, USA, 2004

• Jones, Sue Jenkyn. *Fashion Design*. Laurence King Publishing, London, 2005

• Kyoto Costume Institute. *Fashion History*. Taschen, Cologne and London, 2005

• Laver, James. *Costume and Fashion: a Concise History*. Thames & Hudson, USA, 2002

• López, Ana Maria. *Diseño de moda por ordenador*. Anaya Multimedia, Madrid, 2002

• Martinez Barreiro, Ana. *Mirar y hacerse mirar, la moda en las sociedades modernas*. Editorial Tecnos, 1998

• Pawlik, Johannes. *Theorie der Farbe. Eine Einführung in begriffliche de ästhetischen Farbenlehre*. DuMont, Germany, 1979

• Seeling, Charlotte. *Fashion: the Century of the Designer, 1900–1999*. Konemann, Cologne, 2000

• Tatham, Carolina and Reaman, Julian. *Fashion Design Drawing Course*. Barron's Educational Series, New York, 2003

• Treptouw, Doris. I*nventando moda*. Emporio do livro, Brazil, 2003

Acknowledgements

We wish to thank the Catalan Fashion Institute, its students and ex-students for their valuable and active cooperation on this work, with special thanks to:
Adriana Zalacain, Álex Aragón, Anna Ferrater, Anna Vila, Anouk Puntel, Berta Sesé, David Dolader, David Aducci, Esther Rozas 'Yosolita', Gory de Palma, Irene Vilaseca, Isaac Andrés, Joana Juhé, Laura Bergas, Lola Cuello, Marta Marqués, Noemi Beltrán, Paloma Debatian, Sephora Andrade, Silvia Salaver, Tony Domínguez and Vanessa González.

Thanks to José Luis Sánchez for the hairdressing and make-up, and to the models, Olga and Cristina, for their patience and professionalism.

We also wish to express our sincere appreciation to other contributors whose work and know-how have gone into this book: Laura Fernández, María Botella, Manuel Albarrán, Rafa Mollar and Producciones Grunge.

Finally, we thank Parramón Publishing and particularly María Fernanda Canal for her support and involvement in every phase of this work.